A STUDY
of God's Love & Mankind's History

C. Frank Moore

World rights reserved. This book or any portion thereof may not be copied or reproduced in any form or manner whatever, except as provided by law, without the written permission of the publisher, except by a reviewer who may quote brief passages in a review.

The author assumes full responsibility for the accuracy of all facts and quotations as cited in this book. The opinions expressed in this book are the author's personal views and interpretations, and do not necessarily reflect those of the publisher.

This book is provided with the understanding that the publisher is not engaged in giving spiritual, legal, medical, or other professional advice. If authoritative advice is needed, the reader should seek the counsel of a competent professional.

Copyright © 2014 TEACH Services, Inc.
ISBN-13: 978-1-4796-0438-8 (Paperback)
ISBN-13: 978-1-4796-0420-3 (ePub)
ISBN-13: 978-1-4796-0421-0 (Mobi)
Library of Congress Control Number: 2015931236

All scripture quotations, unless otherwise indicated, are taken from the King James Version. Public domain.

Scripture quotations marked (NIV) are taken from the Holy Bible, New International Version®, NIV®. Copyright © 1973, 1978, 1984, 2011 by Biblica, Inc.™ Used by permission of Zondervan. All rights reserved worldwide.

Published by

TEACH Services, Inc.
P U B L I S H I N G
www.TEACHServices.com • (800) 367-1844

Dedication

The information found in this book is compiled for the honest seeker who is searching the Bible in an effort to understand the Creator God and to develop a relationship with Him and others. This study concerns a Creator God who loves His creation so much that He continually and personally gives correction and guidance (by angels and prophets) to His created beings so they will have right "relationships" and be worthy of His kingdom.

Acknowledgments

First and foremost, to my departed wife, Joyce, who labored with me in this life. Also, this endeavor could not have been completed without the valuable and capable assistance of Pastor Daniel Graham, Murvin Pelto, Ruth M. Swan, and Kalie Kelch. We pray that the information found within these pages will be a light unto your path.

Table of Contents

Dedication 3

Acknowledgments 4

Table of Contents 5

Introduction 7

Chapter 1: The Creator God and Man, His Creation 9

Chapter 2: Man's Rebellion and the Promised Remedy 12

Chapter 3: Worship of the True God 19

Chapter 4: Man's False Worship/Arrogance 24

Chapter 5: The Commonality of Truth Seen in False Beliefs 28

Chapter 6: Things to Come, Previous Revelations 35

Chapter 7: Knowledge and Understanding From the Revelation of Jesus 61

Chapter 8: False Worship/Assembling 75

Chapter 9: Behold, I Come Quickly 91

Chapter 10: Some Misunderstood Teachings 97

Chapter 11: More Misunderstood Terms and Parables 103

Introduction

I have written this book as a companion resource to religious seminars that seek to explore prophecy and the "beliefs/doctrines" taught in the Bible.

Since we are a nation or people who want instant answers and the "bottom line," this will be an abbreviated study of God and His principles and how God relates to mankind, His created beings. More importantly, this book seeks to instill in mankind the desire to maintain a loving, focused relationship with their Creator. Volumes could be written and never exhaust the facts nor thoroughly cover even a fraction of the whole.

Our opinions are based upon the information we receive whether it is from feelings, fears, fantasies, or facts. These opinions then guide all our daily decisions, which is why it is so important that our "database" is filled with correct and truthful information. The purpose of this study is to show you God's unfathomable love and instill in you a desire to have an abiding love relationship with Him. I hope this book also answers questions about why there is so much suffering and hate in the world.

Chapter 1
The Creator God and Man, His Creation

The Bible—The Only True History

First, we need to establish that the Bible is a true history because it is the basis upon which we will derive our foundational information concerning God and the history of mankind's existence. The Bible is a history of God's creation in the heavens and on earth. It is a record of His relationship with His creation and all of creation with Him.

The Bible is comprised of sixty-six books and was written over a span of 1,500 years by approximately thirty-nine different writers (prophets). "All scripture is given by inspiration of God, and is profitable for doctrine, for reproof, for correction, for instruction in righteousness: That the man of God may be perfect, thoroughly furnished unto all good works" (2 Tim. 3:16, 17). God wants to have a close relationship with His created beings, so He gave us the Scriptures that we may get to know Him. Second Peter 1:20, 21 says, "Knowing this first, that no prophecy of the scripture is of any private interpretation. For the prophecy came not in old time by the will of man: but holy men of God spake as they were moved by the Holy Ghost." Looking at the Old Testament concerning this same subject, it reads, "Surely the Lord God will do nothing, but he revealeth his secret unto his servants the prophets" (Amos 3:7).

There are no contradictions in the scriptures, only wrong interpretations. The Holy Spirit gave the same principles/information to all the prophets. The information in the Bible is everlasting and was given so all mankind would see and understand the truth of the "big picture" concerning redemption and salvation of mankind.

Isaiah 8:20 cautions us to test that which we hear: "To the law and to the testimony: if they speak not according to this word, it is because there is no light in them." Scripture teaches us that the method by which God teaches knowledge and understanding of doctrine is by building "precept ... upon precept,

precept upon precept; line upon line, line upon line; here a little, and there a little" (Isa. 28:10). The Bible is full of verses that speak to the importance of studying Scripture (see also 1 Sam. 15:19; Ps. 102:26, 27; Mal. 3:6; Rom. 11:29; and James 1:17):

Search the scriptures; for in them ye think ye have eternal life: and they are they which testify of me. (John 5:39)

Wherefore, beloved, seeing that ye look for such things, be diligent that ye may be found of him in peace, without spot, and blameless. And account that the longsuffering of our Lord is salvation; even as our beloved brother Paul also according to the wisdom given unto him hath written unto you; as also in all his epistles, speaking in them of these things; in which are some things hard to be understood, which they that are unlearned and unstable wrest, as they do also the other scriptures, unto their own destruction. (2 Peter 3:14–16)

There is a way which seemeth right unto a man, but the end thereof are the ways of death. (Prov. 14:12)

For the time will come when they will not endure sound doctrine; but after their own lusts shall they heap to themselves teachers, having itching ears, and they shall turn away their ears from the truth, and shall be turned unto fables. (2 Tim. 4:3, 4)

God is not a man, that he should lie; neither the son of man, that he should repent: hath he said, and shall he not do it? or hath he spoken, and shall he not make it good? (Num. 23:19)

In hope of eternal life, which God, that cannot lie, promised before the world began. (Titus 1:2)

Jesus Christ the same yesterday, and to day, and for ever. (Heb. 13:8)

Establishing Truth

Truth is established by and with two or three witnesses. It is not up to just one person to determine truth. The following scriptures point to this fact:

One witness shall not rise up against a man for any iniquity, or for any sin, in any sin that he sinneth: at the mouth of two witnesses, or at the mouth of three witnesses, shall the matter be established. (Deut. 19:15; see also Deut. 17:6; Matt. 18:16; 2 Cor. 13:1; 1 Tim. 5:19; Heb. 10:28; Rev. 11:3; John 8:17)

That which was from the beginning, which we have heard, which we have seen with our eyes, which we have looked upon, and our hands have handled, of the Word of life; (For the life was manifested, and we have seen it, and bear witness, and shew unto you that eternal life, which was with the Father, and was manifested unto us;) That which we have seen and heard declare we unto you, that ye also may have fellowship with us: and truly our fellowship is with the Father, and with his Son Jesus Christ. (1 John 1:1–3)

In recapitulating, we find that the Holy Spirit was the source that moved the prophets to write the books or records of the happenings that occurred in their day. Each prophet wrote in his own style and language, but the principles that they put on paper are the same. They echoed the same theme—reconciliation to God through the Messiah, Jesus, and obedience to God through love. All were witnesses who testified to God's redemptive plan. To understand a matter, one has to search the scriptures as a whole concerning that matter. Trying to justify our position from texts that we can seemingly manipulate doesn't constitute truth or rightness; instead, it ends in our destruction. God doesn't change His principles or His laws. He doesn't lie. His rule is everlasting. As we just read in Titus 1:2, He "promised [eternal life] before the world began."

Discovering God

Genesis 1:1 says, "In the beginning God created the heaven and the earth." But, let's go further back in time. John 1:1, 3 states, "In the beginning was the Word, and the Word was with God, and the Word was God…. All things were made by him; and without him was not any thing made that was made." Turning back to Genesis, we read, "And the earth was without form, and void; and darkness was upon the face of the deep. And the Spirit of God moved upon the face of the waters…. And God said, Let us make man in our image, after our likeness" (Gen. 1:2, 26).

Our God made us, leads us, and sustains us, just as He led the children of Israel: "For I do not want you to be ignorant of the fact, brothers and sisters, that our ancestors were all under the cloud and that they all passed through the sea … They all ate the same spiritual food and drank the same spiritual drink; for they drank from the spiritual rock that accompanied them, and that rock was Christ" (1 Cor. 10:1–4, NIV).

And He calls us to partner with Him to reach the world: "Go ye therefore, and teach all nations, baptizing them in the name of the Father, and of the Son, and of the Holy Spirit" (Matt. 28:19). In addition to this verse being a call to action, it reminds us that we serve a triune God—three separate individuals in one accord, one purpose, total harmony. And we are invited to be part of that uniqueness.

Jesus, in praying to the Father, said, I pray "that they all may be one; as thou, Father, art in me, and I in thee, that they also may be one in us: that the world may believe that thou hast sent me" (John 17:21). The uniqueness of God is expressed in 1 John 4:8, "He that loveth not knoweth not God; for God is love." The total essence of God is a compilation of character traits that can be condensed down to one word—agape love. John 3:16 confirms this thought: "For God so loved the world, that he gave his only begotten Son, that whosoever believeth in him should not perish, but have everlasting life."

With this pure love emanating throughout heaven, God began His creative work.

Chapter 2
Man's Rebellion and the Promised Remedy

Satan's Evil Schemes

There was peace, tranquility, and joy in heaven until one angel made a choice to rebel against God. Discord did not begin with the Godhead or with God's government, but with one of God's created angels. This angel had remarkable intelligence, outstanding beauty, and held the highest position of honor given to any created being in heaven; however, he began to reason that God's government might not be based on love, but tyrannical power. The record of this is found in Ezckiel 28:2, 11–19, where God asked Ezekiel to write about the king of Tyrus, which was a depiction of Lucifer.

Son of man, say unto the prince of Tyrus, Thus saith the Lord God; Because thine heart is lifted up, and thou hast said, I am a God, I sit in the seat of God, in the midst of the seas; yet thou art a man, and not God, though thou set thine heart as the heart of God: ... Moreover the word of the Lord came unto me, saying, Son of man, take up a lamentation upon the king of Tyrus, and say unto him, Thus saith the Lord God; Thou sealest up the sum, full of wisdom, and perfect in beauty. Thou hast been in Eden the garden of God; every precious stone was thy covering, the sardius, topaz, and the diamond, the beryl, the onyx and the jasper, the sapphire, the emerald, and the carbuncle, and gold: the workmanship of thy tabrets and of thy pipes was prepared in thee in the day that thou was created. Thou art the anointed cherub that covereth; and I have set thee so: thou wast upon the holy mountain of God; thou hast walked up and down in the midst of the stones of fire. Thou wast perfect in thy ways from the day that thou wast created, till iniquity was found in thee. By the multitude of thy merchandise they have filled the midst of thee with violence, and thou hast sinned: therefore ... I will destroy thee, O covering cherub, from the midst of the stones of fire. Thine heart was lifted up because of thy beauty, thou hast corrupted thy wisdom by reason of thy brightness: I will cast thee to the ground, I will lay thee before kings, that they may behold thee. Thou hast defiled thy sanctuaries by the multitude of thine iniquities, by the iniquity of thy traffick; therefore will I bring forth a fire from the midst of thee, it shall devour thee, and I will bring thee to ashes upon the earth in the sight of all them that behold thee. All they that know thee among the people shall be astonished at thee: thou shalt be a terror, and never shalt thou be any more. (Ezek. 28:2, 11–19)

The Old and New Testament document Lucifer's fall from heaven and his banishment to this earth, which he claims as his kingdom.

How art thou fallen from heaven, O Lucifer, son of the morning! how art thou cut down to the ground, which didst weaken the nations! For thou hast said in thine heart, I will ascend into heaven, I will exalt my throne above the stars of God: I will sit also upon the mount of the congregation, in the sides of the north: I will ascend above the heights of the clouds; I will be like the most High. Yet thou shalt be brought down to hell, to the sides of the pit. They that see thee shall narrowly look upon thee, and consider thee, saying, Is this the man that made the earth to tremble, and did shake kingdoms. (Isa. 14:12–16)

And the seventy returned again with joy, saying, Lord, even the devils are subject unto us through thy name. And he said unto them, I beheld Satan as lightning fall from heaven. (Luke 10:17, 18)

And his tail drew the third part of the stars of heaven, and did cast them to the earth ... And there was war in heaven: Michael and his angels fought against the dragon [Rev. 20:2 identifies Satan as the dragon]; and the dragon fought and his angels, and prevailed not; neither was their place found any more in heaven. And the great dragon was cast out, that old serpent, called the Devil, and Satan, which deceiveth the whole world: he was cast out into the earth, and his angels were cast out with him. (Rev. 12:4, 7–9)

Here we see a problem, but we also see that a solution has already been predicted or prophesied. So, what was the problem? From the evidence given, Satan not only questioned, but he challenged God's character, the very principles upon which He exists. He challenged God's love for humanity, which is the foundation of His character. "He that loveth not knoweth not God; for God is love.... And we have known and believed the love that God hath to us. God is love; and he that dwelleth in love dwelleth in God, and God in him" (1 John 4:8, 16). Exodus 34 lists God's attributes: "The Lord, The Lord God, merciful and gracious, longsuffering, and abundant in goodness and truth" (verse 6). "And this is love, that we walk after his commandments. This is the commandment, That, as ye have heard from the beginning, ye should walk in it."

This same love is embodied in the Ten Commandments. The first four commandments speak about our love for God. The last six express our love for our fellow human beings (see Matt. 22:37–40; Deut. 6:5; Lev. 9:18).

Lucifer charge against God was that He was not being the loving God He portrayed Himself to be. We do the same thing when we attempt to justify our wrong actions. Lucifer had, as previously described, remarkable intelligence, outstanding beauty, and power as the leading angel in heaven. He was a perfectly created being. He was not a robot; he was a free-thinking individual. Lucifer had to choose whether he would obey or disobey, follow or lead, worship God or worship self. You and I were created with that same capacity, to think and to choose. Sadly, Lucifer wanted to be like God. Pride overwhelmed him and he sinned against God by desiring to take God's place in His government.

Defining Sin

The following verses help define sin.

Whosoever committeth sin transgresseth also the law: for sin is the transgression of the law. (1 John 3:4)

But sin is not imputed when there is no law. (Rom. 5:13)

What shall we say then? Is the law sin? God forbid. Nay, I had not known sin, but by the law: for I had not known lust, except the law had said, Thou shalt not covet…. Wherefore, the law is holy, and the commandment holy, and just, and good. (Rom. 7:7–12)

If ye fulfill the royal law according to the scripture, Thou shalt love thy neighbor as thyself, ye do well: … For whosoever shall keep the whole law, and yet offend in one point, he is guilty of all. For he that said, Do not commit adultery, said also, Do not kill. Now if thou commit no adultery, yet if thou kill, thou art become a transgressor of the law. So speak ye, and so do, as they that shall be judged by the law of liberty. (James 2:8–12)

For Satan to have been guilty of sin, he had to have transgressed some law. Let's go back over the things he did.

1. He coveted a position that wasn't his.

2. He declared himself to be God, exalting himself above God.

3. He failed to honor his Father and Creator.

4. One-third of the angels paid him homage instead of honoring God.

5. He tried to steal that which belonged to God.

6. By setting himself up to be worshipped, he committed adultery and idol worship. (In Hosea 1:2, God likened the kingdoms of Israel and Judah to a whore.)

7. His portrayal of the Father was through lies; he is said to be the father of lies (John 8:44).

8. He is a murderer. The plan of salvation was put in place before the foundation of the world. His sin killed the Son of God, just as ours did. It is my opinion that Satan and the fallen angels had a chance for redemption also, but pride stopped them from being repentant and obedient.

9. By spreading his lies, he coveted the angels' allegiance.

The evidence is that Satan was guilty of transgressing nine out of the ten commandments that show our love to and for God and to and for our fellow beings. And if you consider the fact that the fourth commandment entails worship, which Satan desires for himself, then all ten commandments were broken.

Mankind's Deception and Decline

Satan's charge against God or challenge to His authority seems to reside in the following acts of rebellion and discontented thinking.

1. The belief that God doesn't really love or there wouldn't be these restrictive and stringent laws.

2. We are intelligent beings capable of making the right decision. Therefore, we should have free reign to think and act as we desire without any restraints or laws.

3. Laws produce forced obedience, not love.

4. Our way is superior to God's way.

5. We are only doing that which we are entitled to.

These seem to be Satan's arguments then, and ours today. Division, deceit, dishonesty, and disobedience are not part of God's plan and do not produce peace and harmony. There is no place in God's universe for these principles, nor for those who ascribe to them.

Where love existed alone, now we have rebellion, selfishness, and evil. God could have eradicated the rebellious beings at the point of instigation, but that would not have erased Satan's accusations. Jude 1:9 says, "Yet Michael the archangel, when contending with the devil he disputed about the body of Moses, durst not bring against him a railing accusation, but said, The Lord rebuke thee." We find other verses that talk about Satan's accusatory nature. Revelation 12:10 states, "The accuser of our brethren is cast down." And 2 Peter 2:4 says, "For if God spared not the angels that sinned, but cast them down to hell, and delivered them into chains of darkness, to be reserved unto judgment." The full results of those accusations have to be totally manifested so that all will be satisfied that Satan's rebellion and claims are false. Just keep that phrase, "reserved unto judgment" in the back of your mind as we continue to unfold these events concerning Satan being cast out of heaven.

Returning to Genesis, let's examine how Satan presented himself to Eve. Remember, everything was perfect. The environment, the animals, the vegetation, and mankind worked in harmony without fear or problems. Perfection reigned in the Garden of Eden. But then Satan entered the picture.

> Now the serpent was more crafty than any of the wild animals the Lord God had made. [Remember, this is a being from heaven using an animal to do his bidding.] He said to the woman, "Did God really say, 'You must not eat from any tree in the garden'?" The woman said to the serpent, "We may eat fruit from the trees in the garden, but God did say, 'You must not eat fruit from the tree that is in the middle of the garden, and you must not touch it, or you will die.'" "You will not certainly die," the serpent said to the woman. "For God knows that when you eat from it your eyes will be opened, and you will be like God, knowing good and evil." When the woman saw that the fruit of

the tree was good for food and pleasing to the eye, and also for gaining wisdom, she took some and ate it. She also gave some to her husband, who was with her, and he ate it. (Gen. 3:1–6, NIV)

Satan did and does what God can't do—lie. He deceives, misrepresents, and casts doubt. None of these methods is meant to uplift or enhance people. His methods are meant to destroy. This was the means by which one-third of the angels were led to leave their heavenly home (Jude 6).

Eve doubted, and she added to God's original command, saying that God told her that she "must not touch it" (Gen. 3:3). Satan capitalized on Eve's overstatement by saying, "Ye shall not surely die," in reference to touching the fruit, another half-truth, for he knew that to eat it she would die. This opened the way for Satan to state the lie and for Eve to doubt God more, by saying, "For God knows that when you eat from it your eyes will be opened, and you will be like God, knowing good and evil" (verse 4, NIV). While Satan is saying this, he most likely had plucked a fruit and had taken a big, juicy bite to prove that nothing happened. "When the woman saw that the fruit of the tree was good for food and pleasing to the eye, and also desirable for gaining wisdom, she took some and ate it" (verse 6, NIV).

Can't you just imagine seeing Satan handing her half of that juicy, beautiful, aromatic fruit? And with a smile that said, I'm freeing you to live your life to the fullest—no restraints—he caused her to fall.

Can We Save Ourselves?

What a difference a day makes, especially in the wake of a wrong choice.

And the eyes of them both were opened, and they knew that they were naked; and they sewed fig leaves together, and made themselves aprons. And they heard the voice of the Lord God ... and ... hid themselves from the presence of the Lord God amongst the trees of the garden. And he [Adam] said, I heard thy voice in the garden, and I was afraid, because I was naked; and I hid myself. (Gen. 3:7–10)

Once God found Adam and Eve, He spoke with them about the consequences, and He offered them the promise of the Redeemer, who would restore all things.

And I will put enmity between thee and the woman, and between thy seed and her seed; it shall bruise thy head and thou shalt bruise his heel. Unto the woman he said, I will greatly multiply thy sorrow and thy conception; in sorrow thou shalt bring forth children ... And unto Adam he said ... cursed is the ground for thy sake; in sorrow shalt thou eat of it all the days of thy life; thorns also and thistles shall it bring forth to thee; and thou shalt eat the herb of the field; in the sweat of thy face shalt thou eat bread, till thou return unto the ground; for out of it wast thou taken: for dust thou art, and unto dust shalt thou return.... Therefore the LORD God sent him forth from the garden of Eden. (Gen. 3:15–23)

Instead of a pleasant, leisurely, happy existence, they now had to live in a harsh environment with thorns, thistles, and drudgery. Instead of eternal life, pain, suffering, and death would now be the norm. Face-to-face communion was lost. The one ray of hope was in the plan of redemption that had already been set in place. Our God, the true God, the Almighty God, the all-knowing God had already made provision for the redemption of mankind.

> And I beheld ... a Lamb as it had been slain ... And they sung a new song, saying, Thou art worthy to take the book, and to open the seals thereof: for thou wast slain, and hast redeemed us to God by thy blood out of every kindred, and tongue, and people, and nation ... Blessing, and honour, and glory, and power, be unto him that sitteth upon the throne, and unto the Lamb for ever and ever. (Rev. 5:6–13)

> Forasmuch as ye know that ye were not redeemed with corruptible things, as silver and gold ... but with the precious blood of Christ, as of a lamb without blemish and without spot: Who verily was foreordained before the foundation of the world, but was manifest in these last times for you. (1 Peter 1:18–20)

> In the hope of eternal life, which God, that cannot lie, promised before the world began. (Titus 1:2)

> Be not thou therefore ashamed of the testimony of our Lord, nor of me his prisoner: but be thou partaker of the afflictions of the gospel according to the power of God; who hath saved us, and called us with an holy calling, not according to our works, but according to his own purpose and grace, which was given us in Christ Jesus before the world began. (2 Tim. 1:8, 9)

> According as he hath chosen us in him before the foundation of the world, that we should be holy and without blame before him in love. (Eph. 1:4)

The first verse of John 17 records Jesus pouring out His heart to the Father in prayer, revealing the relationship and mission of the Son: "Father, the hour is come; glorify thy Son, that thy Son also may glorify thee." The time had come that had been planned for before sin entered the world. Should sin occur God would vindicate and glorify His creation by the glory of Christ's self-sacrificing love. You see, love and peace is the only foundation that will last, and peace is the end product of love.

Adam and Eve saw that they were naked and in their shame they attempted to fix the problem themselves by sewing fig leaves together to hide their nakedness. Their innocence was stripped away by sin. They stood guilty before the Father, and in desperation they tried to hide their guilt by their own works. The penalty for their disobedience was death. They lost their immortality when they chose to disobey God and His principles. Now one must be born again.

Man cannot redeem himself. He can only "pay the price," for "the wages of sin is death," but fortunately, "the gift of God is eternal life through Jesus Christ our Lord" (Rom. 6:23).

The record shows that God clothed Adam and Eve with animal skins, thus the couple witnessed the first death of an innocent living thing for their benefit (Gen. 3:21). Hebrews 9:22 states, "And almost all things are by the law purged with blood; and without shedding of blood is no remission." Turning back to the Old Testament, Leviticus 17:11 says, "For the life of the flesh is in the blood: and I have given it to you upon the altar to make an atonement for your souls: for it is the blood that maketh an atonement for the soul." Immediately following Adam and Eve's act of sin, the promise of salvation and the symbolism of Christ's sacrifice was introduced. From that time forward, God's people maintained the act of sacrificing a perfect Lamb until Christ died on the cross.

Chapter 3
Worship of the True God

True Worship Versus False Worship

Let's begin this chapter by looking at Cain and Abel's sacrifices and the differences between their gifts of worship:

> In the course of time Cain brought some of the fruits of the soil as an offering to the LORD. But Abel also brought an offering—fat portions from some of the firstborn of his flock. The LORD looked with favor on Abel and his offering, but on Cain and his offering he did not look with favor. So Cain was very angry, and his face was downcast. Then the LORD said to Cain, "Why are you angry? Why is your face downcast? If you do what is right, will you not be accepted? But if you do not do what is right, sin is crouching at your door; it desires to have you, but you must rule over it." Now Cain said to is brother Abel, "Let's go out to the field," While they were in the field, Cain attacked his brother Abel and killed him. (Gen. 4:3–8, NIV)

First of all, both Cain and Abel came with offerings to the Lord. They came to worship the Creator God who had given them instructions as to the correct manner to offer sacrifices for their sins. This wasn't an offering of thanksgiving for the bountiful harvest that was given by a merciful, gracious, and loving God, because God in His questioning indicated that Cain knew what the right offering was to be.

Who, also, was outside the garden of Eden? Satan! Shades of rebellious history! We find anger, discontent, pride, rebellion, envy, hate, and finally murder. God could have killed Cain then and there, but Satan's rebellion has to run its full course. It has to be fully and forever seen for what it is and its end results. Therefore, Cain, like Lucifer, was driven out of the land after he acted on his rebellion.

The account recorded in Genesis indicates that Cain's behavior was not acceptable, but by recognizing his sin, he could have been restored.

Sadly, the record also indicates that Cain's pride hardened his rebellious heart to the point of murder. We are admonished to "harden not your heart" (Ps. 95:8; see also Heb. 3:8, 15; 4:7). Instead, let us worship God in spirit and in truth (John 4:24).

Preserving the Truth

Now we shall move ahead in time, but we will continue our study of God's prescribed plan of worship as contrasted with Satan's. In this fifth chapter of Genesis, we find the age and genealogy of the descendants of Adam to Noah. In the midst of the list, we read about Enoch, who only lived 365 years, for he was taken to heaven by God without dying because of his close association and worship of God. Elijah experienced the same fate (2 Kings 2:11). These two men are symbolic of the righteous who will be gathered to heaven at Christ's second coming without seeing death.

Cain's descendants did not worship God, but Seth's descendants did. There were ten generations from Adam to Noah, and by simple calculation of this genealogy, it is interesting and important to note that truth was established by the two-or-three-witness rule. There is a span of 1,656 years from creation (Adam's birth) to the flood. Adam lived 930 years. Adam lived with Enoch for 295 years; with Methuselah for 238 years; and with Lamech for fifty-one years. Noah lived with Methuselah and Lamech approximately 600 years; and Shem lived with them for approximately 100 years.

After the flood Noah lived for 450 years, and Shem for 500 years. Abraham lived 175 years. Therefore, Abraham was alive for fifty years while Noah was, and he died thirty-five years before Shem died. Abraham learned about God through the stories that were passed down from Noah and Shem after the flood, but he had to have faith to fully trust in God, which we know was accounted to him as righteousness.

By faith Abraham, when he was called to go out into a place which he should after receive for an inheritance, obeyed; and he went out, not knowing whither he went. By faith he sojourned in the land of promise, as in a strange country, dwelling in tabernacles with Isaac and Jacob, the heirs with him of the same promise: for he looked for a city which hath foundations, whose builder and maker is God.... These all died in faith, not having received the promises, but having seen them afar off, and were persuaded of them, and embraced them, and confessed that they were strangers and pilgrims on earth.... By faith Abraham, when he was tried, offered up Isaac: and he that had received the promises offered up his only begotten son, of whom it was said, That in Isaac shall thy seed be called: accounting that God was able to raise him up, even from the dead; from whence also he received him in a figure. (Heb. 11:8–19)

The act of Abraham being willing to sacrifice Isaac pointed forward to the sacrifice that God would make, offering His own Son on the cross to save us of our sins.

The Tower of Babel

Let's return to the events following the flood. From the eight persons who were saved, there was to be a new beginning. "And the LORD said unto Noah, Come thou and all thy house into the ark; for thee have I seen righteous before me in this generation" (Gen. 7:1). But what about the rest of earth's population? "And God saw that the wickedness of man was great in the earth, and that every imagination of the thoughts of his heart was only evil continually.... And the LORD said, I will destroy ... for all flesh had corrupted his way upon the earth" (Gen. 6:5, 7, 12).

Now here are eight persons who have just experienced how corrupt the earth and its inhabitants had become and witnessed how God viewed such actions by His judgmental wrath. But, they also witnessed His love, grace, longsuffering, and mercy in saving them and representatives of all species of animals. "And Noah builded an altar unto the LORD" (Gen. 8:20), and upon that altar, Noah sacrificed clean animals and birds in thanks to God. Mankind had been redeemed from death because of their belief and obedience to God.

But the cleansing of the earth from its wickedness did not last long. Genesis 9:21–29 tells the sad account of the continued presence of sin and the poor choices that even God's servant Noah made. The Bible documents the fact that Noah got drunk and was naked in his tent. Ham found him in that condition, and he goes and tells his two brothers. We are not given further details of the incident, but Ham's actions resulted in he and his descendants being cursed by Noah, with servitude to his brothers.

The Scattering of the Nations

Genesis 10 gives the genealogies of Noah's three sons; and chapter 11 tells the account of the tower of Babel and the confounding of the common language to various languages. "Then they said, 'Come, let us build ourselves a city, with a tower that reaches to the heavens, so that we may make a name for ourselves; otherwise we will be scattered over the face of the whole earth'" (Gen. 11:4, NIV).

Genesis 10:25 talks about a man named Eber who had two sons: "the name of one was Peleg; for in his days was the earth divided." We can calculate that Peleg's birth was 1,756 years after creation and 100 years after the flood. Looking at Noah's other descendants, we read about Ham's grandson Nimrod, the mighty hunter, who built Babel (or Babylon). Nimrod built the city when God had said to Noah and his sons, "Be fruitful, and multiply, and replenish the earth" (Gen. 9:1), which was the same instruction He had given Adam and Eve (Gen. 1:28).

Please notice that the construction of the city and tower were the beginning of Nimrod's kingdom. By saying, "Let us build" or "let us make," they were leaving God out of the equation. They desired to construct a tower that would reach to heaven and put them where God is. They desired to make a name for themselves instead of living as sons of God. In John 5:44, Jesus said, "How can ye believe, which receive honour one of another, and seek not the honour that cometh from God only?"

Notice, also, that the same methods Satan used in the Garden of Eden are again present here in the disobedience of Nimrod—the lust of the flesh, the lust of the eyes, and the pride of life. The people were scattered and their language was confounded or made different. However, a most important fact to remember is that whatever ideas these people chose to believe about God, it was now scattered throughout the whole earth. All the world's inhabitants at that time, through the families of Noah and his three sons, had been made aware of the true creator God. Each nation, clan, group, culture, family, or individual person passed their genetic makeup to those with the same genetic pool.

Mankind and All Things Are Fearfully and Wonderfully Made

The various characteristics of each race were developed as the people spread out throughout the world, and yet everyone came from Noah and his family's lineage after the flood. Acts 17:24–27 puts it this way, "God that made the world and all things therein ... hath made of one blood all nations of men for to dwell on all the face of the earth, and hath determined the times before appointed, and the bounds of their habitation; that they should seek the Lord, if haply they might feel after him, and find him, though he be not far from every one of us."

Today scientists report that the DNA sequence of humans is about 99.9 percent identical throughout the world. Isn't it amazing? The Bible holds the answers that support this scientific finding. They discover what God said is true from the beginning, approximately 6,000 years ago. Man "begat" man, and since the flood the gene pools that were passed from Noah and his wife to their sons and grandchildren has been passed to the rest of the human family.

Just as we found the genealogic record to be scanty on details from Adam to Noah, so we find the history from Noah to Abraham, and also, in our study from Abraham to the Messiah, the Promised One, the Redeemer and Savior of the world. However, we do find the thread of lineage is through Shem to Abraham, then on down through Isaac to Jacob, and continuing through Judah to Jesse, and lastly through David to Mary and Joseph and ending with Jesus. No, Joseph wasn't Jesus' earthly father. However, both Mary and Joseph's lineage was through David (Isa. 7:14; Luke 1:26–35; Matt. 1:1–16; and Luke 3:23–38).

Worshipping the True God or False Gods

With the scattering of the nations, there was also a dividing of the world into two major camps: the followers of God and the followers of false gods. To say "I don't believe there is any God or gods" is to set one's self up as god; and therefore, that person aligns himself or herself with Satan, for he said, "I will exalt my throne above the stars of God" (Isa. 14:13). To worship anything that one has made is to set oneself in the place of God as creator of an idol. Even one who worships and acknowledges that God is God but is not obedient to His word is not offering true worship to the Creator. Jesus told the Pharisees and scribes in Matthew 15:7–9: "Ye hypocrites, well did Esaias [Isa. 29:13] prophesy of you, saying, This people draweth nigh unto me with their mouth, and honoureth me with their lips; but their heart is far from me. But in vain they do worship me, teaching for doctrines the commandments of men." The second group is God's true followers, those who have chosen to acknowledge Him as the living Creator. They are totally committed to Him and are obedient to His calling.

You cannot "straddle the fence" or "live in the best of both worlds" by trying to serve God and self (or other things). We are either totally His or totally on Satan's side. It is no real mystery when one truly investigates the matter to discover that Satan is at the root of all that is evil in this world, and so many have chosen to follow him.

When we look around and contemplate the "why's" of life and search for the meaning of our existence, we must turn to Scripture for the real answers. We must also recognize that we will never know everything there is to know about the universe, nor do not need to know. The main thing we need to keep at the forefront of our mind is that God is love. He created everything, and in that sense He is in everything. The one thing He did not create is evil, for that characteristic is in direct opposition to His very nature. Isaiah 45:7 seems to be contradictory to this point until one understands that God uses those things which God had warned against in bringing disobedient mankind to repentance. Evil is opposite to that which is good.

Again, let's pull some of the loose threads to a conclusion. We have discussed that all things were created by and for God and His pleasure. Adam walked and talked with God in the Garden of Eden. Enoch walked with God and was taken to heaven without dying. The seventh-day Sabbath was sanctified by God, not just as a memorial of creation but as a time of fellowship between man and his Creator (Gen. 2:1–3; Lev. 1:1–3).

As long as the Sabbath was observed, which pointed to the Creator, there was no room for false worship or evolution. Romans 1:18–20 tells us that "the wrath of God is revealed from heaven against all ungodliness and unrighteousness of man, who hold the truth in unrighteousness; because that which may be known of God is manifest in them; for God hath shewed it unto them. For the invisible things of him from the creation of the world are clearly seen, being understood by the things that are made, even his eternal power and Godhead; so that they are without excuse." Eight verses later Paul wrote, "And even as they did not like to retain God in their knowledge, God gave them over to a reprobate mind [void of judgment]" (verse 28).

We have learned that each plant and animal reproduces "after his kind." Therefore, we can safely say that God, who doesn't lie and who created all things, knows the subject of genetics thoroughly and can be trusted when He says He created man and all living things. Darwin's theory of evolution cannot overcome the laws that govern DNA in nature. Nature doesn't manipulate from species to species; but, man, through Satan, does. We must not forget the power Satan has! He was once in a high and honored position in heaven, and he still possesses great power. It is only by eliminating God, by denying His existence, or separating Him from His created beings that Satan can propagate his false ideas.

If we believe Satan's lies about evolution, life has no purpose, no meaning, no future! Over time knowledge has been expanded, but to what end? The microscopic world hasn't been and cannot be controlled. We, the human race, continue to die earlier, even with advanced technology on our side. Scientists are working on ways to achieve longer life expectations; however, the only means for attaining this goal is to believe in God and accept the assurance of salvation. Unfortunately, many would rather believe in scientists who promise miracle drugs to extend life rather than place their trust in the Creator of the universe. Scientists may alter the life that God created, but they cannot produce life from nothing as God did. I choose to place my future and my faith on the history that is recorded in the Bible.

Chapter 4
Man's False Worship/Arrogance

Religious Differences—Different Belief Systems

At this point, let's explore the various and widely different philosophies concerning the worship of a god or the true God. Each of us needs to closely evaluate our beliefs to see if they follow the Word of God or the commandments of men. We will be going more in depth as we study a number of the doctrines, teachings, and instructions given by God that have been twisted by man and accepted as God's word. This study will only show the leading religious beliefs of the world in contrast to the instructions given by God concerning the correct way to live life and worship Him. Each person must decide which philosophy to follow, that of God or that of Satan.

As previously seen, there was a scattering of the earth's inhabitants that occurred in approximately 2249 BC. According to the record given, Noah lived for 450 years after the flood, and Shem lived for 500 years after the flood. Therefore, they were alive when the tower of Babel was constructed and the languages were confounded, for this event took place 100 years after the flood. All living persons at that time knew or should have known about the true God and the flood. But as we know, Satan deceives earth's inhabitants anyway he can. This is the world that Abraham was born into. Remember, Noah and Shem were still alive when Abraham was an adult, which brings us to his story.

Abraham's Calling

"Now the LORD had said unto Abram, Get thee out of thy country, and from thy kindred, and from thy father's house, unto a land that I will shew thee: And I will make of thee a great nation, and I will bless thee, and make thy name great; and thou shalt be a blessing: and I will bless them that bless thee, and curse him that curseth thee: and in thee shall all families of the earth be blessed" (Gen. 12:1–3).

Years later Joshua urged the children of Israel to choose whom they would serve, whether it be the God of Abraham or the gods of the Amorites.

> And Joshua gathered all the tribes of Israel to Shechem ... and Joshua said unto all the people, Thus saith the LORD God of Israel, Your fathers dwelt on the other side of flood in old time, even Terah, the father of Abraham, and the father of Nachor: and they served other gods....
>
> Now therefore fear the LORD, and serve him in sincerity and in truth: and put away the gods which your fathers served on the other side of the flood, and in Egypt; and serve ye the LORD. And if it seem evil unto you to serve the LORD, choose you this day whom ye will serve; whether the gods which your fathers served that were on the other side of the flood, or the gods of the Amorites, in whose land ye dwell: but as for me and my house, we will serve the LORD. (Josh. 24:1, 2, 14, 15)

We have seen time after time the consequences of not following the truth—Satan's rebellion, the deception of Adam and Eve, the flood, the idolatry of Israel—but the children of Israel were free to make their own decision as to whom they would serve, just as we are free today. Through it all, God remained faithful, merciful, longsuffering, and encouraging to those who were loyal to His principles.

Our Examples/Admonition

Paul wrote concerning these events that happened approximately 1,500 years before his time and 3,500 years before our time: "Now all these things happened unto them for ensamples: and they are written for our admonition, upon whom the ends of the world are come" (1 Cor. 10:11).

Through the events of the Bible, we are witnesses to God's character in action. He is gracious, righteous, just, and abundant in goodness and truth. We are also witnesses to the byproducts of disobedience. God is love; and peace comes with obedience. God chose seventy-five–year-old Abraham to be the father of a great nation, and he obeyed by faith and left his country and the idolatrous practices of his father. This was fifteen years after Noah's death, twenty-five years before Isaac's birth, and approximately 1,983 years before Christ was born. It was also approximately 266 years after the scattering of the nations, therefore, giving us a time frame for the coming events.

God, who cannot lie, said in Genesis 17:19–21, "Sarah thy wife shall bear thee a son indeed; and thou shalt call his name Isaac: and I will establish my covenant with him for an everlasting covenant, and with his seed after him. And as for Ishmael, I have heard thee: Behold, I have blessed him, and will make him fruitful, and will multiply him exceedingly; twelve princes shall he beget, and I will make him a great nation. But my covenant will I establish with Isaac, which Sarah shall bear unto thee at this set time next year."

Claiming the Promised Land

Many years later God's chosen people, the seed of Abraham, began to inhabit the land God had promised to give them. Noah and his family had been saved because of their faith and obedience to God. Abraham, too, had been faithful to God and had been blessed because of his allegiance to his

Creator. However, as the kingdoms of Israel were set up in the Promised Land, tribe by tribe, they faltered in their loyalty to God. "And also all that generation were gathered unto their fathers: and there arose another generation after them, which knew not the LORD, nor yet the works which he had done for Israel. And the children of Israel did evil in the sight of the LORD, and served Baalim: ... And they forsook the LORD, and served Baal and Ashtaroth" (Judges 2:10–13).

The biggest problem was that the children of Israel did not drive the inhabitants out according to God's directions. Therefore, there were ongoing conflicts with the surrounding nations, and their cultural practices influenced the Israelites. As long as Israel obeyed, there was peace. When Israel disobeyed, there was conflict. "And it came to pass, when the judge was dead, that they returned, and corrupted themselves more than their fathers, in following other gods to serve them, and to bow down unto them; they ceased not from their own doings, nor from their stubborn way" (Judges 2:19). *"In those days there was no king in Israel, but every man did that which was right in his own eyes"* (Judges 17:6, emphasis added). Isn't that similar to how people operate today? Everyone does his or her own thing?

Moses warned the people about the dangers of conforming to the nations around them, but they still fell prey to Satan's temptations.

> But ye that did cleave unto the LORD your God are alive every one of you this day. Behold, I have taught you statutes and judgments, even as the LORD my God commanded me, that ye should do so in the land whither ye go to possess it. Keep therefore and do them; for this is your wisdom and your understanding in the sight of the nations, which shall hear all these statutes, and say, Surely this great nation is a wise and understanding people. For what nation is there so great, who hath God so nigh unto them, as the LORD our God is in all things that we call upon him for? And what nation is there so great, that hath statutes and judgments so righteous as all this law, which I set before you this day? Only take heed to thyself, and keep thy soul diligently, lest thou forget the things which thine eyes have seen, and lest they depart from thy heart all the days of thy life: but teach them thy sons, and thy sons' sons. (Deut. 4:4–9; see Josh. 22:5)

There failed not ought of any good thing which the LORD had spoken unto the house of Israel; all came to pass. (Josh. 21:45)

The Lord is not slack concerning his promises, as some men count slackness; but is longsuffering to us-ward, not willing that any should perish, but that all should come to repentance. (2 Peter 3:9)

The Promised Land was strategically located to fulfill God's purpose for Israel, which was to enlighten all peoples of earth and share with them the message of salvation. It was at the crossroads of the then-known world, and God intended that the Israelites would share the goods news with the Gentiles: "And the Gentiles shall come to thy light, and kings to the brightness of thy rising" (Isa. 60:3); "And in that day there shall be a root of Jesse, which shall stand for an ensign of the people; to it shall the Gentiles seek: and his rest shall be glorious" (Isa. 11:10).

This is predictive of Jesus and the gospel. God's chosen people, Israel, vacillated between doing right and doing evil. This resulted in peaceful periods giving away to disobedience and times of enemy oppression and exile. It is clear that obedience to the principles, laws, and will of God by His people leads to righteousness and peace.

Chapter 5
The Commonality of Truth Seen in False Beliefs

Is There a Common Origin for Beliefs

Now let's jump ahead, past Israel's years of slavery in Egypt as God told Abraham would happen (Gen. 15:13–16), to King Solomon's time, which was approximately 1168 BC, and the beginning of the building of the temple. The following texts give us insight into Solomon's reign.

And God gave Solomon wisdom and understanding exceeding much, and largeness of heart ... And Solomon's wisdom excelled the wisdom of all the children of the east country ["But unto the sons of the concubines, which Abraham had, Abraham gave gifts, and sent them away ... unto the east country" (Gen. 25:6)], and all the wisdom of Egypt. For he was wiser than all men; ... and his fame was in all nations round about.... And there came of all people to hear the wisdom of Solomon, from all kings of the earth, which had heard of his wisdom. (1 Kings 4:29–34)

And when the queen of Sheba heard of the fame of Solomon concerning the name of the LORD, she came to prove him with hard questions. (1 Kings 10:1)

And she said to the king, It was a true report which I heard in mine own land of thine acts, and of thy wisdom: ... and, behold, the one half of the greatness of thy wisdom was not told me: for thou exceedest the fame that I heard. (2 Chron. 9:5, 6)

And he spake three thousand proverbs: and his songs were a thousand and five. (1 Kings 4:32)

Happy are thy men, happy are these thy servants, which stand continually before thee, and that hear thy wisdom. (1 Kings 10:8)

For the king had at sea a navy of Tharshish with the navy of Hiram: once in three years came the navy of Tharshish, bringing gold, and silver, ivory, and apes, and peacocks. So king Solomon exceeded all the kings of the earth for riches and for wisdom. And all the earth sought to Solomon, to hear his wisdom, which God had put in his heart. (1 Kings 10:22–24)

As these verses demonstrate, Solomon's wisdom and fame spread to all kings of the earth. Some form or knowledge of the true creator God was scattered to all the earth's inhabitants. We do not know how far these families traveled before they established themselves in the land, or how rapidly they spread as far as the land extended. Through the fame of Solomon, knowledge of the true God and His principles went to the known world. Solomon's navy probably traveled at least as far as Southwest India, and perhaps, to the Spice Islands of Indonesia.

The Oriental Philosophies— Tainted Versions of God's Principles

Why is this of interest? When we consider the beginnings of certain beliefs or religious philosophies, especially as they have to do with man's relationship to God or a god and to mankind, it is good to see if there is a common thread or origin for those beliefs or practices. I obtained the following information concerning the beliefs of the Hindu, Buddha, Confucian, and Islam religions from the 1970 volume of the *Encyclopedia Britannia* and various websites for the individual religions.

Hindu

This religion is thought to have formed around 1,000 BC, and became more evolved about 600 BC. Its beliefs consist of:

1. Karma (law of cause and effect). Each individual creates his own destiny.
2. Divinity of the *vedas* (scripture) and hymns.
3. One supreme being (creator and unmanifest reality).
4. Universe (endless cycles of creation, preservation, dissolution).
5. Reincarnation of the soul to eventual *moksha* (all conflicts resolved).
6. Divine beings exist in unseen worlds (devas and gods).
7. A spiritual awakened master or *satguru* is essential to know the transcendent absolute.
8. All life is sacred—"non injury."
9. No particular religion teaches the only way to salvation above all others. All genuine religious paths are facets of god's pure love and light, deserving tolerance and understanding.

Buddhism

Buddha was thought to be born in 563 BC in Northern India. He was born the son of a king, but it is believed that he renounced his nobility. It is said that he was knowledgeable of both Hindu and Asceticism, but rejected both. He didn't claim to be a god, but he held to wisdom that was "enlightenment from within." Buddha taught, "for you art Buddha." "How to live the good life" was the goal. He taught that we should love our neighbors and all things. Some of his other teachings were to not kill, steal, not lie, not get intoxicated, and not have illicit sex. The Noble Eightfold Path has to do with correct "understanding, thoughts, speech, action, livelihood, effort, mindfulness, and concentration." The *duhhka* (lust) has to be brought to an end; therefore, reincarnation is a main belief because one must live again until one gets it right.

Confucianism

The following paragraphs provide insight into Confucianism from the *Encyclopedia Britannica*:

"Confucius is the Latinized name of "Kong Fuzi," which means Master Kong, an honorary title. He was born in 551 BC and became an educator/reformer. His teachings sought to shape the individual into a man of perfect virtue who wanted to establish his own character and also help others to establish character.

"The two clearly divergent tendencies that developed was represented by great learning (social and political in nature) that aims at manifesting one's clear character, loving the people, and abiding in the highest good. This was to be accomplished by the "eight steps of (1) investigation of things, (2) extension of knowledge, (3) sincerity of will, (4) rectifying the mind, (5) cultivating the personal life, (6) regulating the family, (7) ordering the state, and (8) bring peace to the world.

"The second tendency, the doctrine of the mean was religious and metaphysical interpreting Confucius' doctrine of the mean to central harmony. That is, the full realization of self through the harmony of the emotions, and the development and operation of all things in harmonious relationships. Underlying all this is sincerity, which, as the way of all existence, is absolute, intelligent, and indestructible. Only those who are absolutely sincere can develop fully their own natures, the natures of other people, the nature of things, and finally partake in the creative work of heaven and earth.

"Confucianism was not regarded as a religion. Though it promoted the traditions of heaven, the sacred mountains and rivers, and ancestors, its supremacy lay in the secular realm." "Virtue is to love men, and wisdom is to understand men." "Confucius regarded mankind as one large family." "The truly virtuous man, desiring to be established himself, seeks to establish others: Desiring success for himself, he strives to help others succeed. To find in the wishes of one's own heart the principle for his conduct toward others is the method of true virtue" ("Confucianism," *Encyclopedia Britannica,* vol. 6 [1970], pp. 305–310).

It is not the scope of this study to present or explore all the false "ways" Satan has diverted the attention of the population of this world away from God, but let's look at these three teachings as an entity, since they have a lot in common, and compare them with the historical record we have established thus far.

First, let's look at the timing. Solomon's reign and writings, along with the Queen of Sheba's visit and that of other kings, took place around 1100 BC or earlier. Therefore, the Lord God, creator of heaven and earth, had already given these principles or teachings to the "scattered" inhabitants through Solomon's writings and by word of mouth along the trade routes that extended to the known world.

Hinduism had its beginnings approximately 1,250 years after the Tower of Babel experience and 100 or more years after Solomon's reign. Buddhism and Confucianism were introduced hundreds of years later, but before the Babylonian Empire captured Israel, and subsequently the rest of the world. This was about 527 BC as found in Daniel 9:24–27 and Ezra 6:14. Even though a foreign king was in power, God still introduced him to His way. King Nebuchadnezzar acknowledged that Daniel's God was the true God (Dan. 2:47). And King Darius declared, "I make a decree, that in every dominion of my kingdom men tremble and fear the God of Daniel: for he is the living God, and stedfast for ever, and his kingdom that which shall not be destroyed, and his dominion shall be even unto the end" (Dan. 6:26).

What are the principles of the true God? We have found that God is love. Love is a manifestation of God's character. We have seen before that He is merciful, gracious, longsuffering, abundant in goodness and truth, just, and that all His characteristics are summed up in the Ten Commandments. The first four deal with our love to and for God. The last six deal with our love to and for our fellow human beings. They are the essence of "do unto others as you would have others do unto you." Therefore, we can readily see that these three religions had their foundation in the truths that had been given by God to His people, but Satan distorted the heavenly teachings. Satan's original lies to Eve, "You will not die, and you will be like God," are major tenants of these false religions. It is true that these religions contain some right principles and right virtue, but there is the worm in the apple.

With these philosophies, it is the "self" that "self" is trying to get rid of/correct; yet, it is the "self" that "self" is trying to elevate. As we saw with the antediluvians, their thoughts were continually evil. The fig leaves were not a covering for the breach that occurred with disobedience. The penalty was and is death. Therefore, "self" cannot of "self" attain that which requires "one's" life, for one to secure life means that the penalty has to be born by another. No matter how many times one could be reincarnated, one would still have to pay the penalty. The penalty is death, not eternal life by endless reincarnations and not just physical, but spiritual death also.

As we have seen, Scripture gives the solution, for before the foundation of the earth a plan was in place that, if necessary, the Lamb of God would die to save humanity. He, God's Son, paid the price that should have been yours and mine. It is our choice whether we will accept this gift of God. The only strings attached are a total surrender of self and obedience to God. Isn't that the underlying principle of these three philosophies, the "right" type of life? But eternal life can't be obtained, since we can never pay the penalty and still have life in ourselves. The answers must come as planned by the Creator—Jesus' substitutionary death.

A Look at Islam

Now, let's explore the main points of a philosophy/religion that has more recently come into the spotlight, Islam. It was propagated by the prophet Mohammed who was born in AD 622, and it means "surrender to God's will." The Koran is proposed to be the word of God, "confirming and consummating the earlier revealed books and thereby replacing them" (Josh McDowell and John Gilchrist, *The Islam Debate* [San Bernardino, CA: Here's Life Publishers, 1983], p. 23) There are five beliefs: (1) one God (absolute), (2) angels, (3) in the revealed books, (4) in the

Prophets, and (5) in the Day of Judgment. To be a Muslim, one has to repeat and believe the *shahada*, which states, "There is no god but God, Mohammed is the messenger of God." There are five pillars (obligatory duties): (1) repeating the profession of faith (*shahada*), (2) prayers, (3) paying the *zahat* tax, (4) fasting, and (5) making a pilgrimage to Mecca during one's life, if possible.

I confess that I have not read the Koran in full, but this information was gathered from the official Islam website and the *Encyclopedia Britannia*. It is notable that it does not say that God does not lie. Why is this important? The earlier revealed books that the Koran is supposed to have replaced clearly state that God cannot lie and that He is the same yesterday, today, and forever. If there is a statement in the Koran that God does not lie, then the Koran, by replacing the earlier prophets' writings, has made God a liar. The act of replacing these writings in itself causes God to be a liar. Either way, the Koran is not the "thus saith the Lord God."

The prophets of the Bible all spoke or wrote in harmony concerning God's spoken word to them in their dealings with the human family and with God's principles, laws, statutes, and prophecies. There are no contradictions since the Holy Spirit gave the same to all. If Mohammed had been a true prophet, the Koran would confirm the words of God spoken to the other prophets and written on the tablets of stone. But Islam rejects that God created the Sabbath by resting on the seventh day. This is in direct conflict with the Genesis account (Gen. 2:1–3) and Moses' account of God writing the Ten Commandments on the two tablets of stone with His own finger. The fourth commandment is the remembrance of the seventh day: "But the seventh day is the sabbath of the Lord thy God … For in six days the Lord made heaven and earth, the sea, and all that in them is, and rested the seventh day: wherefore the Lord blessed the sabbath day, and hallowed it" (Exod. 20:10, 11).

Doesn't it seem strange that the fourth belief of Islam concerns believing in the prophets and messengers of God, including Adam, Noah, Abraham, Ishmael, Isaac, Jacob, Moses, and Jesus, according to their list, but that the writings from the biblical prophets, as previously given via a true witness, have been twisted or denied in the Koran by a person claiming to be a prophet?

This reminds me of the story in 1 Kings 13. A true prophet of God listened to and obeyed the lies of "a prophet also as thou art" (verse 18).

The Koran and Mohammed are circuitous. According to Islamic belief, in order for salvation, one has to believe Allah and his prophet and the Koran, which was authored by Mohammed, his prophet. But if Mohammed was illiterate as was reported, who wrote the Koran? Also, consider this. Within the Koran Mohammed denounced the validity of the true word of God and Jesus as the Son of God; thereby, discrediting God's plan of salvation. It is stated that the angel Gabriel instructed Mohammed in the writing of the Koran. This is, supposedly, the same Gabriel who was sent to Daniel with the message of the longest time prophecy, which foretold the time of the birth of the Messiah. The same Gabriel that was sent to Zacharias and to Mary with the predictive messages concerning the soon birth of their sons. Zacharias and his wife were old, and Elizabeth was barren, but the prophecy was fulfilled, and their son prepared the way for the Messiah. To Mary, Gabriel gave the message that she was to be the honored woman that every woman since

Eve had dreamed to be—the mother of the Messiah. As predicted, she was a virgin. The Child (Jesus) did not have an earthly father but was conceived by the Holy Spirit, as was also predicted. He is the Son of the heavenly Father.

Would Gabriel tell Mohammad that the messages he had delivered more than 600 years previously were false? Null? Void? Would Gabriel say that all the messages that God had given to His prophets were void? In other words, would the true Gabriel call God a liar? Let's get some insight or scriptural knowledge of who Gabriel is/was.

Turning to 1 Samuel 28:7–19, we find the story of King Saul visiting a "woman that hath a familiar spirit" to bring up Samuel so that he could receive instruction from him. We know that it wasn't Samuel who appeared, but this event underscores the fact that Satan and his evil angels can and do manifest themselves as God's true messengers.

Paul wrote, "For such are false apostles, deceitful workers, transforming themselves into the apostles of Christ.... whose end shall be according to their works" (2 Cor. 11:13–15). Based on this information, it is clear that the angel who visited Mohammad was sent by Satan.

My fellow searcher for truth, God did not and does not lead His chosen (elect) people or honest seekers through vast trials and tribulations that Satan sets and then abandon them to false beliefs. Satan did not deny that God was God to Eve, but he surely lied to her in order to seduce her into disobedience. "Woe unto them that call evil good, and good evil; that put darkness for light, and light for darkness; that put bitter for sweet, and sweet for bitter!" (Isa. 5:20).

From his time in heaven until now, Satan has tried to thwart the righteous government of God. Look at the numerous examples already given in this study, and there will be more as we continue. This is just another of the many simultaneous efforts to divert allegiance from the true God and His plan of salvation. Will you believe God or the "wolf in sheep's clothing"? Your eternal life depends upon your choice. None of these philosophies give credence to God's plan for man's redemption, which is to restore one to perfect peace with God through love and by Jesus' sacrifice.

Peter answered rightly, when Jesus asked His disciples who people were saying he was. "Simon Peter answered and said, Thou art the Christ, the Son of the living God. And Jesus answered and said unto him, Blessed art thou, Simon Barjona: for flesh and blood hath not revealed it unto thee, but my Father which is in heaven" (Matt. 16:16, 17; see also Mark 8:28, 29). Jesus acknowledged that He is the Christ (the Messiah, the Promised One, the Redeemer for whom the world was looking) and that He is the Son of the heavenly Father. Jesus said in Matthew 10:33, "But whosoever shall deny me before men, him will I also deny before my Father which is in heaven."

God and His principles and characteristics have not changed, nor do they need to change. He and they will remain the same from everlasting to everlasting. It is we, His creation, who need to change our attitudes and ideas, which have been subtly eroded by the false influences of Satanic forces. It is only by diligent study that the wisdom and true understanding of our standing before God can be appreciated, and if we do not reject the enlightenment we receive by and through the Holy Spirit, we will be able to walk before the Lord, our God, with a humble and contrite heart.

The record is clear. We must follow the sacred instructions that are open for all to see and understand in order to restore ourselves and others to the original path that God had set before the world began. Satan will cast doubt, distort facts, and do all types of miraculous things (illusions) in his attempt to convince us that his way (disobedience) is correct. God did not arbitrarily cast Satan out of heaven. Satan chose the path he took, which was contrary to the pure, holy, true, righteous, gracious, merciful, just, and longsuffering standards that are God's character. We need to return to the original path.

We have continued to see God's leading and man's hot and cold attitude in choosing to follow the "way." Isaiah 29:13 and Matthew 15:7–9 well characterize man's relationship with God, saying, "Ye hypocrites, well did Esaias prophesy of you, saying, This people draweth nigh unto me with their mouths and honoureth me with their lips; but their heart is far from me. But in vain they do worship me, teaching for doctrines the commandments of men."

Chapter 6
Things to Come, Previous Revelations

The Prophecies of Daniel

We have seen that the rise of these "isms" occurred before the Babylonian captivity of Israel, and we will now study God's involvement in the affairs of all men. This has been seen in the past dealings with, not only Israel, but all nations of earth. Since the books of Daniel and Revelation are prophetic of God's future plans for mankind, let's explore them to discover what's ahead and what He expects, as well as some of His doctrines.

> And Isaiah said unto [King] Hezekiah, Hear the word of the LORD.... And of thy sons that shall issue from thee, which thou shall beget, shall they take away; and they shall be eunuchs in the palace of the king of Babylon. (2 Kings 20:16, 18)

> And the king spake unto Ashpenaz the master of his eunuchs, that he should bring certain of the children of Israel, and of the king's seed, and of the princes; Children in whom was no blemish, but well favoured, and skilful in all wisdom, and cunning in knowledge, and understanding science, and such as had ability in them to stand in the king's palace, and whom they might teach the learning and the tongue of the Chaldeans. And the king appointed them a daily provision of the king's meat, and of the wine which he drank: so nourishing them three years, that at the end thereof they might stand before the king. Now among these were of the children of Judah, Daniel, Hananiah, Mishael, and Azariah: ... But Daniel purposed in his heart that he would not defile himself with the portion of the king's meat, nor with the wine which he drank: therefore he requested of the prince of the eunuchs that he might not defile himself. (Dan. 1:3–8)

Diet—Clean Versus Unclean Foods

> Daniel then said to the guard ... "Please test your servants for ten days: Give us

nothing but vegetables to eat and water to drink. Then compare our appearance with that of the young men who eat the royal food ..." At the end of the ten days they looked healthier and better nourished than any of the young men who ate the royal food. (Dan. 1:11–15, NIV)

Daniel was concerned that he would defile his body by eating the food offered to them. What food did God provide or allow to be eaten? Are there instructions for what we should eat? When were these guidelines given? Were these restrictions ever done away with?

Here's what we find in the Garden of Eden: "Then God said, 'I give you every seed-bearing plant on the face of the whole earth and every tree that has fruit with seed in it. They will be yours for food. And to all the beasts of the earth and all the birds in the sky and all the creatures that move along the ground—everything that has the breath of life in it—I give every green plant for food.' And it was so" (Gen. 1:29, 30, NIV).

We note that this was the diet of the people and animals until the flood, which was calculated through the genealogies of Adam's descendants to have been 1,656 years from creation.

God told Noah to enter the ark and "take thou unto thee of all food that is eaten, and thou shalt gather it to thee; and it shall be for food for thee, and for them" (Gen. 6:21). Here we notice that there has been no change in diet. It is "of all food that is eaten." As we proceed to Genesis 7:2, 3, we find some distinctions in the classification of the animals into clean and unclean groupings. "Of every clean beast thou shalt take to thee by sevens, the male and his female: and of beasts that are not clean by two, the male and his female. Of the fowls also of the air by sevens, the male and the female; to keep seed alive upon the face of all the earth."

Why is this distinction important? On disembarking the ark, " Noah built an altar unto the Lord; and took of every clean beast, and of every clean fowl, and offered burnt offerings on the altar" (Gen. 8:20). Then God said to Noah concerning the animals, all of which had been friendly to Noah, "And the fear of you and the dread of you shall be upon every beast of the earth, and upon every fowl of the air, upon all that moveth upon the earth, and upon all the fishes of the sea; into your hand are they delivered. Every moving thing that liveth shall be meat for you; even as the green herb have I given you all things. But flesh with the life thereof, which is the blood thereof, shall ye not eat" (Gen. 9:2–4).

Because God cannot lie, it is important to fully understand what God is saying in the previous statement in regards to diet. What is His intent in the words "every moving thing that liveth shall be meat for you; even as the green herb have I given you all things"? When looking back at Genesis 1:29, 30, it wasn't "all" plants that were created which were considered edible for humans or animals, but those which bore seed.

God had instructed the clean and unclean animals to be brought into the ark by specific numbers of pairs. Why? For several reasons, first, it had to do with the manner of worshipping God. "And almost all things are by the law purged with blood; and without shedding of blood is no remission" (Heb. 9:22). Jesus said in Matthew 26:28: "For this is my blood of the new testament, which is shed for many for the remission of sins." Again, the plan of salvation has remained the same from before the foundation of the world—Christ, the slain Lamb of

God, is who saves us (John 1:29; Rev. 5:6; 13:8). Only clean animals are to be offered as a sacrifice to God, for they represent Christ.

The unclean animals were not to be touched and were never intended to be consumed by mankind as food. "Moreover the soul that shall touch any unclean thing, as the uncleanness of man, or any unclean beast, or any abominable unclean thing, and eat of the flesh of the sacrifice of peace offerings, which pertain unto the Lord, even that soul shall be cut off from his people" (Lev. 7:21; see also verses 18–20).

Leviticus 11 and Deuteronomy 14 tell of the clean animals that were edible and the unclean animals that were not to be eaten. "And the Lord spake unto Moses and to Aaron, saying unto them, Speak unto the children of Israel, saying, These are the beasts which ye shall eat among all the beasts that are on the earth" (Lev. 11:1, 2).

Notice that these instructions were given to two witnesses that it should be truly established. The children of Israel had complained about the food and desired the "flesh pots of Egypt." There should have been no question of clean and unclean, since those guidelines had been established approximately 800 years earlier at the time of the flood. However, the children of Israel had been in bondage in Egypt for a great number of years—although they were a few people when they went into Egypt voluntarily and free, they soon were oppressed and forced into slavery, which had been predicted years before—and had not retained the close walk they should have. Therefore, they needed to be reminded of God's expectations of them individually. That is why God spent forty days with Moses on Mount Sinai, re-establishing His principles by the giving and writing of all His instructions.

Another thing concerning unclean animals is that they are the scavengers of earth. Their job is to keep the earth free of debris whether vegetable or animal. Again, they were never intended for human consumption.

Satan's formula for "right living" is self above all, pride, lies, oppression, greed, and no restrictive laws. It was the evil ambitions of the Pharaoh "that knew not Joseph," that resulted in the slavery of the children of Israel. However, they were God's chosen people.

> For thou art an holy people unto the LORD thy God: the LORD thy God hath chosen thee to be a special people unto himself, above all people that are upon the face of the earth. The LORD did not set his love upon you, nor choose you, because ye were more in number than any people; for ye were the fewest of all people: But because the LORD loved you, and because he would keep the oath which he had sworn unto your fathers, hath the LORD brought you out with a mighty hand, and redeemed you out of the house of bondmen, from the hand of Pharaoh king of Egypt. (Deut. 7:6–8)

Remember, it was to Abraham and his seed that God chose to be a blessing to "all families of the earth" (Gen. 12:3).

One Law for All God's People

There is something else that is important to note about this "chosen people":

> All that are born of the country shall do these things after this manner ... And if a stranger sojourn with you ... as ye do, so he shall do. One ordinance shall be both

for you of the congregation, and also for the stranger that sojourneth with you, an ordinance for ever in your generations: as ye are, so shall the stranger be before the LORD. One law and one manner shall be for you, and for the stranger that sojourneth with you. (Num. 15:13–16)

The Lord our God is one God. He is the same yesterday, today, and forever. His chosen people were to spread His word and knowledge of Him to all the world, that all would be blessed of Him. His laws, commandments, statutes, and ordinances are true and to be obeyed by all His people. It is recognized that there were certain ritual and ceremonial laws that were for a limited time because they were symbolic of Christ's redemptive work as the Messiah. God makes no distinction between the believer who was of Israel and the believing sojourner in the Old Testament, and the same guidelines apply in the New Testament. Galatians 3:28, 29 tells us that "there is neither Jew nor Greek, there is neither bond nor free, there is neither male nor female: for ye are all one in Christ Jesus. And if ye be Christ's, then are ye Abraham's seed, and heirs according to the promise."

The argument that the dietary laws were just for the Israelites is false. If a person claims to believe and follow God, then God's dietary laws should be part of his or her commitment to God, as it was with Daniel when he purposed in his heart not to defile his body.

Paul wrote in 1 Corinthians 3:16, 17, "Know ye not that ye are the temple of God, and that the Spirit of God dwelleth in you? If any man defile the temple of God, him shall God destroy; For the temple of God is holy, which temple ye are" (see also 1 Cor. 6:19, 20).

Some have tried to use Peter's vision of the sheet in Acts 10 and Paul's discussion of judging in Romans 14 as evidence that these passages cleaned the unclean animals and that, in our Christian "freedom," it is admissible to eat anything. At first reading it sounds like the claim is true, yet on careful examination the true explanation is missed in all of these accounts.

There is a saying that I once heard that illustrates this type of thinking. It is this, "As long as sin is persisted in, man will search for a way to vindicate his continuing therein." If one falls into this trap, it would be good to remember Peter's statement in 2 Peter 3:16: "As also in all his [Paul] epistles, speaking in them of these things; in which are some things hard to be understood, which they that are unlearned and unstable wrest, as they do also the other scriptures, unto their own destruction."

Paul wrote the following to Titus: "To the pure, all things are pure, but to those who are corrupted and do not believe, nothing is pure. In fact, both their minds and consciences are corrupted. They claim to know God, but by their actions they deny him. They are detestable, disobedient and unfit for doing anything good" (1:15, 16, NIV).

Romans 14 has been quoted by those who are being used of Satan to discount many of God's truths through perversion of the scriptures. Again, it must be brought to remembrance, God does not lie nor is there "a shadow of turning with God."

If there is a seeming discrepancy, then scripture concerning the subject is to be the determining factor, not what man chooses the interpretation to be. Therefore, it is impossible for there to have been a cleansing of the unclean animals to make them acceptable for food now. Why do I say that? Look at what Isaiah says, "For, behold, the Lord will come with fire ... For by fire and by his sword will the Lord plead with all flesh: and the slain of the Lord shall be many. They that sanctify themselves, and purify themselves in the gardens behind one tree in the midst, eating swine's flesh, and the abomination, and the mouse, shall be consumed together, saith the Lord" (Isa. 66:15–17).

Now let's look at some texts in the New Testament: "And then shall that Wicked be revealed, whom the Lord shall consume with the spirit of his mouth, and shall destroy with the brightness of his coming" (2 Thess. 2:8). "But the day of the Lord will come as a thief in the night; in which the heavens shall pass away with a great noise, and the elements shall melt with fervent heat, the earth also and the works that are therein shall be burned up" (2 Peter 3:10).

We can plainly see from creation to the end of this world that there is a diet that God has prescribed and that will be carried on even in the new heavens and new earth for all created beings. If the dietary laws were abandoned as some claim, picture this scene in the new earth where the redeemed from all ages are seated at a table with every description of food from all sources. Moses turns to Isaiah and points to Peter and Paul and says, "Satan was right; God doesn't mean what He says and has double standards."

King Nebuchadnezzar's Dream— World Kingdoms (Empires)

Let's rejoin Daniel because this is a very important book and chapter in giving a foundation for understanding the future, the end of the world, the kingdoms that would rule the then-known world, and the foundation for the rest of the events and chapters in the book of Daniel, as well as a key understanding of the book of Revelation. We will be studying these books together.

The players in Daniel 2 are King Nebuchadnezzar, his magicians, astrologers, sorcerers, the Chaldeans, and later Daniel and his three companions. The king had dreamed a dream, but he couldn't remember it. He was very perturbed and wanted to know the meaning of the dream. His magicians and astrologers could not reveal the dream and, therefore, were ordered to be put to death. Since Daniel and his companions were lumped into this group, they were to be slain also. However, when Daniel was made aware of the decree and the "thing" to be known, he went to the king and asked to be given time so that he could show the king the interpretation.

Daniel and his three companions desired "mercies of the God of heaven concerning this secret" (Dan. 2:18), "then was the secret revealed unto Daniel in a night vision" (verse 19). And "Daniel answered and said, Blessed be the name of God for ever and ever: for wisdom and might are his: And he changeth the times and the seasons: he removeth kings, and setteth up kings: he giveth wisdom unto the wise, and knowledge to them that know and understanding: He revealeth the deep and secret things: he knoweth what is in the darkness, and the light dwelleth with him" (verse 20–22). We are reminded of God's promise that "surely the Lord God will do nothing, but he revealeth his secret unto his servants the prophets" (Amos 3:7).

God's plan of salvation and the path that His people should take, along with the events to take place, have all been revealed throughout the history of man. We must recognize that this dream is not only to Nebuchadnezzar but is for God's people to the end of this earth's history. What was the dream and its interpretation? We can read about it in Daniel 2:26–49:

The king answered and said to Daniel …

Art thou able to make known unto me the dream which I have seen, and the interpretation thereof? Daniel answered … The secret which the king hath demanded cannot the wise men, the astrologers, the magicians, the soothsayers, shew unto the king; But there is a God in heaven that revealeth secrets, and maketh known to the king Nebuchadnezzar what shall be in the latter days. Thy dream, and the visions … are these; As for thee, O King, thy thoughts came into thy mind upon thy bed, what should come to pass hereafter: and he that revealeth secrets maketh known to thee what shall come to pass. (Dan. 2:26–29)

Daniel made it clear that what God said would come to pass. The children of Israel's captivity is proof that what God says will happen, does happen. Daniel continues, "But as for me, this secret is not revealed to me for any wisdom that I have more than any living, but for their sakes that shall make known the interpretation to the king, and that thou mightest know the thoughts of thy heart" (verse 30).

Daniel is admitting that he has no greater power than the "wise men" of the king's court. He makes it clear that the interpretation is not his, but was given of God that King Nebuchadnezzar "might know the thoughts of his heart." The dream was as follows:

Thou, O king, sawest, and behold a great image. This great image, whose brightness was excellent, stood before thee; and the form thereof was terrible. This image's head was of fine gold, his breast and arms of silver, his belly and thighs of brass, his legs of iron, his feet part of iron and part of clay. Thou sawest till a stone was cut out without hands, which smote the image upon his feet that were of iron and clay, and brake them to pieces. Then was the iron, the clay, the brass, the silver, and the gold, broken to pieces together, and became like chaff of the summer threshingfloors; and the wind carried them away, that no place was found for them: and the stone that smote the image became a great mountain, and filled the whole earth.

This is the dream; and we will tell the interpretation thereof before the king. Thou, O King, art a king of kings: for the God of heaven hath given thee a kingdom, power, and strength, and glory. And wheresoever the children of men dwell, the beasts of the field and the fowls of the heaven hath he given into thine hand, and hath made thee ruler over them all. Thou art this head of gold. And after thee shall arise another kingdom inferior to thee, and another third kingdom of brass, which shall bear rule over all the earth. And the fourth kingdom shall be strong as iron: forasmuch as iron breaketh in pieces and subdueth all things: and as iron that breaketh all these, shall it break in pieces and bruise. And whereas thou sawest the feet and toes, part of potters' clay, and part of iron, the kingdom shall be divided; but there shall be in it of the strength of the iron, forasmuch as thou sawest the iron mixed with miry clay. And as the toes of the feet were part of iron and part of clay, so the kingdom shall be partly strong, and partly broken. And whereas thou sawest iron mixed with miry clay, they shall mingle themselves with the seed of men; but they shall not cleave one to another, even as iron is not mixed with clay.

And in the days of these kings shall the God of heaven set up a kingdom, which shall never be destroyed: and the kingdom shall not be left to other people, but it shall break in pieces and consume all these kingdoms, and it shall stand for ever. Forasmuch as thou sawest that the stone was cut out of the mountain without hands, and that it brake in pieces the iron, the brass, the clay, the silver, and the gold; the great God hath made known to the king what shall come to pass hereafter: and the dream is certain, and the interpretation thereof sure.... [Then] the king answered unto Daniel, and said, Of a truth it is, that your God is a God of gods, and a Lord of kings, and a revealer of secrets, seeing thou couldest reveal this secret. (verses 31–47)

King Nebuchadnezzar then made Daniel "ruler over the whole province of Babylon" and "chief of governors over all the wise men" (verse 48). His companions were set "over the affairs of the province of Babylon" (verse 49).

Did this happen? Has there been four "kingdoms" that have ruled over the then-known earth? Yes, and we shall explore this dream in more detail to see how the events of the dream have impacted God's chosen people then and down through the pages of history. From history we will discover that the fulfillment of God's predictions was verified. There have been four world-dominating kingdoms that have ruled the known world. God's chosen people have been under the control of these world kingdoms since their Babylonian captivity until the state of Israel was formed in 1948.

Worship of the Golden Image—False Worship

It is important to note that Nebuchadnezzar didn't dispose of his gods, but he did admit that Daniel's God is "a God of gods, and a Lord of kings." As we move into Daniel 3, we find that King Nebuchadnezzar apparently felt he could make his kingdom last forever. He set up an image entirely of gold on the plain of Dura, in the province of Babylon. It was ninety feet tall and nine feet wide.

Then Nebuchadnezzar the king sent to gather together the princes, the governors, and the captains, the judges, the treasurers, the counsellors, the sheriffs, and all the rulers of the provinces, to come to the dedication of the image ... [all] were gathered together ... before that image Nebuchadnezzar had set up. Then an herald cried aloud, ... at what time ye hear the sound of the comet, flute, harp, sackbut, psaltery, dulcimer, and all kinds of musick, ye fall down and worship the golden image that Nebuchadnezzar the king hath set up: And whoso falleth not down and worshippeth shall the same hour be cast into the midst of a burning fiery furnace.

Therefore, at that time, when all the people heard the sound of ... all kinds of musick, all the people, the nations, and the languages, fell down and worshipped the golden image ... Wherefore at that time certain Chaldeans came near, and accused the Jews. They spake and said to the king Nebuchadnezzar ... There are certain Jews whom thou hast set over the affairs of the province of Babylon, Shadrach, Meshach, and Abednego; these men, O king, have not regarded thee: they serve not thy gods, nor worship the golden image ... Then Nebuchadnezzar in his rage and fury commanded to bring Shadrach, Meshach, and Abednego.... Nebuchadnezzar spake and said unto them, Is it true ... do not ye serve my gods, nor worship the golden image which I have set up? Now if ye be ready that at what time ye hear the sound of ... musick, ye fall down and worship ... ; well: but if ye worship not, ye shall be cast ... into the midst of a burning fiery furnace; and who is that God that shall deliver you out of my hands? (verses 2–15)

Let's stop here for a moment and put what we have learned into proper perspective. We know that Nebuchadnezzar's dream was during the second year of his reign. We don't know how long it took to build the image. We do know that these "captives" were ten times smarter than the Chaldeans and that they were given high government positions instead of the Chaldeans. We know from the severity of the penalty that Nebuchadnezzar's decree to worship the image was a test of loyalty to him and a way to destroy those who by strength and disobedience might seek to overthrow him. He was informed in the interpreting of his dream that another kingdom would overthrow his kingdom; therefore, any insubordination to the king would be a sign of a lack of respect. It's in these types of situations that Satan employs those whose intentions are to trip up and harm God's children.

The enemies of His people are eager to employ such. The king felt the fury of being used by the Chaldeans, and at the same time, his decree was not being honored by these captives, these officials that he had placed over the province.

At this point, let's go to a parallel situation that will most likely occur in our lifetime and involve us. John records the following in Revelation 13:14, 15, "And deceiveth them that dwell on the earth by the means of those miracles which he had power to do in the sight of the beast; saying to them that dwell on the earth, that they should make an image to the beast, which had the wound by the sword, and did live. And he had power to give life unto the image of the beast, that the image of the beast should both speak, and cause that as many as would not worship the image of the beast should be killed."

In both cases, an image was made and men were to worship it rather than the true God or they would be put to death. We will be developing this at a later period, but just remember that this whole study centers on one's choice to worship the true God or some false image god, whether voluntarily or under the threat of death. I have made the commitment to obey and follow the true God. What is your choice?

Continuing now with the story, we read:

Then was Nebuchadnezzar full of fury, and the form of his visage was changed against Shadrach, Meshach, and Abednego: therefore he spake, and commanded that they should heat the furnace one seven times more than it was wont to be heated. And he commanded the most mighty men that were in his army to bind ... and cast them into the burning fiery furnace. Then these [three] men were bound in their coats, their hosen, and their hats, and their other garments, and were cast into the midst of the burning fiery furnace. Therefore because the king's commandment was urgent, and the furnace exceeding hot, the flames of the fire slew those men that took up Shadrach, Meshach, and Abednego. And these three men ... fell down bound into the midst of the burning fiery furnace.

Then Nebuchadnezzar the king was astonished, and rose up in haste, and spake, and said unto his counsellers, Did not we cast three men bound into the midst of the fire? They answered and said unto the king, True, O king. He answered and said, Lo, I see four men loose, walking in the midst of the fire, and they have no hurt; and the form of the fourth is like the Son of God. Then Nebuchadnezzar came near to the mouth of the ... furnace, and spake, and said, ... ye servants of the most high God, come forth, and come hither....

And the princes, governors, and captains, and the king's counsellers, being gathered together, saw these men, upon whose bodies the fire had no power, nor was an hair of their head singed, neither were their coats changed, nor the smell of fire had passed on them. Then Nebuchadnezzar spake, and said, Blessed be the God of Shadrach, Meshach, and Abednego, who hath sent his angel, and delivered his servants that trusted in him, and have changed the king's word, and yielded their bodies, that they might not serve nor worship any god, except their own God. Therefore, I make a decree, That every people, nation, and language, which speak any thing amiss against the God of Shadrach, Meshach, and Abednego, shall be cut in pieces, and their houses shall be made a dunghill: because there is no other God that can deliver after this sort. (Dan. 3:19–29)

This is the second manifestation of the true God's power to Nebuchadnezzar, who was impressed enough to send a decree to the ends of the then-known world that there is a true God. But as we have seen, heart change and a change in actions are from within, and not as a result of men's decrees. However, just visualize all those officials from all of the kingdoms and provinces not only witnessing this miracle of God, but taking the king's decree back to their respective provinces to acknowledge that there is a God greater than any so-called god.

As we explore Daniel 4, we find King Nebuchadnezzar still not converted or convinced that the true God is the only God and it is through Him that "we live, and move, and have our being" (Acts 17:28, see also Col. 1:17; Heb. 1:3). The king has had another dream, and this chapter gives us his confession and latest experience. "Nebuchadnezzar the king, unto all people, nations, and languages, that dwell in all the earth; Peace be multiplied unto you. I thought it good to shew the signs and wonders that the high God hath wrought toward me. How great are his signs! and how mighty are his wonders! his kingdom is an everlasting kingdom, and his dominion is from generation to generation" (Dan. 4:1–3).

End of Nebuchadnezzar's Reign—Dream of the Great Tree

What was the dream and the fulfillment of it that caused this ruler of the "world" to make such a statement and to reverse his arrogance of any god that could reverse his decrees? We have just witnessed the protective power of God concerning the three Hebrews in the fiery furnace. Now let's examine Nebuchadnezzar's latest dream.

I saw, and behold a tree in the midst of the earth, and the height thereof was great. The tree grew, and was strong, and the height thereof reached unto heaven, and the sight thereof to the end of all the earth: The leaves thereof were fair, and the fruit thereof much, and in it was meat for all: the beasts of the field had shadow under it, and the fowls of the heaven dwelt in the boughs thereof, and all flesh was fed of it.... and, behold, a watcher and an holy one came down from heaven; He cried aloud, and said thus, Hew down the tree, and cut off his branches, shake off his leaves, and scatter his fruit: let the beasts get from under it, and the fowls from his branches: Nevertheless leave the stump of his roots in the earth, even with a band of iron and brass, in the tender grass of the field; and let it be wet with the dew of heaven, and let his portion be with the beasts in the grass of the earth: Let his heart be changed from man's, and let a beast's heart be given unto him; and let seven times pass over him. This matter is by the decree of the watchers, and the demand by the word of the holy ones: to the intent that the living may know that the most High ruleth in the kingdom of men, and giveth it to whomsoever he will, and setteth up over it the basest of men. (verses 10–17)

Nebuchadnezzar told Daniel the dream and asked him to interpret it. For an hour Daniel did not know how to tell the king the meaning. It was only with the king's prodding that he spoke, for the king said, "let not the dream, or the interpretation thereof, trouble thee" (verse 19). It's like a good friend saying, "I've got some bad news to tell you, but it's for your own good." That was the situation Daniel found himself in.

Daniel said,

My lord, the dream be to them that hate thee, and the interpretation thereof to thine enemies. The tree that thou sawest ... It is thou, O king ... And whereas the king saw a watcher and an holy one coming down from heaven ... O king, and this is the decree of the most High, which is come upon my lord the king: That they shall drive thee from men, and thy dwelling shall be with the beasts of the field, and they shall make thee to eat grass as an oxen, and they shall wet thee with the dew of heaven, and seven times shall pass over thee, till thou know that the most High ruleth in the kingdom of men, and giveth it to whomsoever he will. And whereas they commanded to leave the stump of the tree roots; thy kingdom shall be sure unto thee, after that thou shalt have known that the heavens do rule. (verses 19–26)

Daniel gives some wise counsel that is ignored. "Wherefore, O king, let my counsel be acceptable unto thee, and break off thy sins by righteousness, and thine iniquities by shewing mercy to the poor; if it may be a lengthening of thy tranquility" (verse 27).

For one year after the dream, Nebuchadnezzar's life remained the same. Nothing that had been predicted had occurred.

At the end of twelve months he walked in the palace of the kingdom of Babylon. [The hanging gardens of Babylon are said to be one of the seven wonders of the world.] The king spake, and said, Is not this great Babylon, that I have built for the house of the kingdom by the might of my power, and for the honour of my majesty? While the word was in the king's mouth, there fell a voice from heaven, saying, O king Nebuchadnezzar, to thee it is spoken; The kingdom is departed from thee.... The same hour was the thing fulfilled upon

Nebuchadnezzar: ... And at the end of the days I Nebuchadnezzar lifted up mine eyes unto heaven, and mine understanding returned unto me, and I blessed the most High, and I praised and honoured him that liveth for ever, whose dominion is an everlasting dominion, and his kingdom is from generation to generation: And all the inhabitants of the earth are reputed as nothing: and he doeth according to his will in the army of heaven, and among the inhabitants of the earth: and none can stay his hand, or say unto him, What doest thou? At the same time my reason returned to me ... Now I Nebuchadnezzar praise and extol and honour the King of heaven, all whose works are truth, and his ways judgment: and those that walk in pride he is able to abase. (verses 29–37)

What true principles of right living do we find in this chapter? The principle of Romans 8:28 applies: "And we know that all things work together for good to them that love God, to them who are the called according to his purpose." It does not matter if it's Joseph going into Egypt (Gen. 50:20) or Pharaoh as the children of Israel left Egypt (Exod. 9:16)—the point is that God is in charge. His purpose and will is carried to completion. Pride led to disobedience in Satan's life and that has been passed on to the human race. It is God's purpose to restore the harmony that this disobedience destroyed. Nebuchadnezzar, who really did not know God (but knew of Him), became the instrument by which knowledge of the true God was sent into all the world. Nebuchadnezzar, in his pride, looked upon his accomplishments and power, and he reveled in his own self-esteem as he pondered the great Babylon, his kingdom, much as Lucifer did in heaven.

It is important to remember the wise words of Solomon: "Pride goeth before destruction, and an haughty spirit before a fall" (Prov. 16:18). "The fear of the Lord is to hate evil: pride: and arrogancy, and the evil way, and the froward mouth, do I hate" (Prov. 8:13). "These six things doth the Lord hate: yea, seven are an abomination unto him: A proud look, a lying tongue, and hands that shed innocent blood, an heart that deviseth wicked imaginations, feet that be swift in running to mischief, a false witness that speaketh lies, and he that soweth discord among brethren" (Prov. 6:16–19).

All these reflect Satan's character and the principles that are esteemed correct by those who follow him. Remember to "seek ye first the kingdom of God, and his righteousness; and all these things [the necessities of life] shall be added unto you" (Matt. 6:33). What are some of the characteristics and principles of following the true God, other than the Ten Commandments? Paul wrote, "But the fruit of the Spirit is love, joy, peace, longsuffering, gentleness, goodness, faith, meekness, temperance" (Gal. 5:22, 23) "and truth" (Eph. 5:9).

We find that Daniel and his companions obeyed the civil laws of the land they were in, but they did not obey laws that conflicted with a "thus saith the Lord." Obedience to the true God comes first. Paul wrote, "Let every soul be subject unto the higher powers. For there is no power but of God: the powers that be are ordained of God" (Rom. 13:1). Jesus said, "Render therefore unto Caesar the things which are Caesar's; and unto God the things that are God's" (Matt. 22:21). God still sets up kingdoms. Did Nebuchadnezzar fully renounce his gods and follow the true God for the rest of his life? We do not know. Daniel is silent regarding his remaining life. What do you think your reaction and choice would have been if you were King Nebuchadnezzar?

At this point in the book of Daniel, it is difficult to know how to proceed since the time sequences of the remaining chapters are not in order and the events portrayed are only slightly related. However, there is no problem with understanding the events or accounts given in these chapters. Belshazzar's first year on the throne is recorded in chapter 7, the third year in chapter 8, and the last year in chapter 5. Then we have the first year of Darius's reign as king of the Medes in chapters 6, 9, 11, and 12. Lastly, we have the third year of Cyrus's reign as king of the Persians in chapter 10.

Daniel in the Lion's Den

Let's continue with the subject of worship as seen in Daniel 6. However, we need to set the stage by understanding a little background history. We learned in chapter 2 that the successions of kingdoms indicated that the Medes/Persians would conquer Babylon. When Darius, the Mede, took charge of the kingdom, he divided it into 120 provinces with a prince over each province. These were to report to the three presidents, which Darius had appointed, and Daniel was chosen to be one, as well as the chief. Jealousy caused the other presidents and princes to plot to get rid of Daniel. However, they could find no fault with Daniel's civil duties and sought to discredit him through or by his religious faith. It was Daniel's custom to pray, with his window open toward Jerusalem, three times a day. The record states:

> Then these presidents and princes assembled together to the king, and said thus unto him, King Darius, live for ever. All the presidents of the kingdom, the governors. and the princes, the counsellers, and the captains, have consulted together to establish a royal statute, and to make a firm decree, that whosoever shall ask a petition of any God or man for thirty days, save of thee, O king, he shall be cast into the den of lions. Now, O king, establish the decree, and sign the writing, that it be not changed, according to the law of the Medes and Persians, which altereth not. Wherefore king Darius signed the writing and the decree. (Dan. 6:6–9)

Do you understand what just occurred? The political intrigue of today goes back to Daniel, Eden, and the corruption and rebellion of one-third of the angels. The subtly and half- truths of Satan were put before a trusting king. He was skillfully guided into signing a decree, which, had he known their motives, he would not have signed. This new king apparently had a lot of information and faith concerning Daniel's ability and integrity to give him the first presidency position with all its inherent power.

A lot of laws are on the books today because someone was able to persuade a "leader" that this law is for the good of the people. Just another example of what will happen when the legislation regarding the mark of the beast will be signed. The people will believe the worship to be worthy of adoration, but in reality the worship will be false worship. And unsuspecting people will be duped again by Satan, just as King Darius was!

We find that Daniel was true to his convictions and customs even in the face of danger. "He kneeled upon his knees three times a day, and prayed, and gave thanks before his God, as he did aforetime" (verse 10). Those men knew they would not need 30 days for Daniel to break this civil law. Are you and I as committed to God as he was? When Daniel's accusers came to the king for enforcement of the law, the record shows that the king "was sore displeased with himself, and set his heart on Daniel to deliver him: and he laboured till the going down of the sun to deliver him" (verse 14).

Then those who had the king sign the decree said, "No decree nor statute which the king establisheth may be changed" (verse 15). Darius, the king, was caught in the trap that these men had set, so he ordered Daniel to be thrown into the lion's den, but not before confessing to Daniel, "Thy God whom thou servest continually, he will deliver thee" (verse 16).

Darius had, no doubt, heard of the experience of the fiery furnace. These conspirators may have even been witness to the miracle of the three Hebrews. It is written that the king spent the night fasting and without music. He didn't sleep; instead, he arose early in the morning and went in haste to the lion's den.

> He cried with a lamentable voice unto Daniel: and the king spake and said to Daniel, O Daniel, servant of the living God, is thy God, whom thou servest continually, able to deliver thee from the lions? Then said Daniel unto the King, O king, live for ever. My God hath sent his angel, and hath shut the lions' mouths, that they have not hurt me ... And the king commanded, and they brought those men which had accused Daniel, and they cast them into the den of lions, them, their children and their wives ... I make a decree, That in every dominion of my kingdom men tremble and fear before the God of Daniel: *for he is the living God*. (Dan. 6:20–26)

It is interesting to note that King Darius is the son of King Ahasuerus (Dan. 9:1) and that Esther became King Ahasuerus' queen whose palace was in Shushan— and who reigned "from India even unto Ethiopia, over an hundred and seven and twenty provinces" (Esther 1:1, 2). Daniel was in Shushan in the place during the third year of king Belshazzar's reign. The enemies of Daniel were cast to the lions, where they met their fate; similarly, Haman, Mordecai's enemy, was hanged on the gallows that he had built for Mordecai. God's justice will always prevail. As we read in the first book of the Bible, God said of His chosen people, "I will bless them that bless thee, and curse him that curseth thee" (Gen. 12:3). Was Darius a believer?

In spite of Israel's disobedience as a whole, there has always been a remnant who have stood firm for God's right principles. We find examples of this in Joseph, Moses, Joshua and Caleb, David, Daniel and his three companions, Elijah, the apostles, the martyrs during the throwing of the Christians to the lions, the Waldenses, and those who were burned at the stake. John records this truth in Revelation 12: "And the dragon was wroth with the woman, and went to make war with the remnant of her seed, which keep the commandments of God, and have the testimony of Jesus Christ" (verse 17). This last group of God's chosen people will be representative of all the redeemed of all ages who "overcome" through faith and obedience (see Rev. 2:7, 11, 17, 26; Rev. 3:5, 12, 21).

The "Overcomer"—The True Israelite

Let's go back to Jacob for a moment and get some important insight into what is meant by "overcomer." It was in God's dealings with

Jacob and Jacob's resolve that "the LORD be my God" (Gen. 28:21) that led eventually to him wrestling with God. "And Jacob called the name of the place Peniel: for I have seen God face to face, and my life is preserved" (Gen. 32:30). "And he said, Thy name shall be called no more Jacob, but Israel: for as a prince hast thou power with God and with men, and hast prevailed" (verse 28). Israel, then, is an overcomer.

We do not overcome by our own merits, but by the blessing or grace of God. "And I heard a loud voice saying in heaven, Now is come salvation, and strength, and the kingdom of our God, and the power of his Christ: for the accuser or our brethren is cast down, which accused them before our God day and night. And they overcame him by the blood of the Lamb, and by the word of their testimony; and they loved not their lives unto the death" (Rev. 12:10, 11).

Paul wrote to the Romans: "Who are Israelites; to whom pertaineth the adoption, and the glory, and the covenants, and the giving of the law, and the service of God, and the promises; ... For they are not all Israel, which are of Israel: Neither, because they are seed of Abraham, are they all children: ... That is, They which are children of the flesh, these are not the children of God: but the children of the promise are counted for the seed" (Rom. 9:4–8).

In the next chapter, Paul wrote "For the scripture saith, [Isa. 28:16] Whosoever believeth on him shall not be ashamed. For there is no difference between the Jew and the Greek: for the same Lord over all is rich unto all that call upon him. For whosoever shall call upon the name of the Lord shall be saved" (Rom. 10:11–13). Along this same theme, he wrote in Galatians: "For ye are all the children of God by faith in Christ Jesus. For as many of you as have been baptized into Christ have put on Christ. There is neither Jew nor Greek, there is neither bond nor free, there is neither male nor female: for ye are all one in Christ Jesus. And if ye be Christ's, then are ye Abraham's seed, and heirs according to the promise" (Gal. 3:26–29).

Isn't that wonderful news! Everyone who chooses to follow God can be His child. All it takes is obedience to His will and word.

Turning back to Daniel, chapter 7, we read about a dream that God sent directly to Daniel. This took place in the first year of King Belshazzar's reign (this is either Nebuchadnezzar's son or grandson). Some years have passed since Nebuchadnezzar had his dream that represented the earth's dominating kingdoms to the end of this world. Daniel's dream fills in the details concerning these powers and how they will affect God's people. So let's begin with the dream, but take note that this dream troubled Daniel to such an extent that the events that are portrayed and predicted are given in chapters 8 through 12. Since these events concerned a great period of time, Daniel was told to "shut up the words, and seal the book, even to the time of the end: many shall run to and fro, and knowledge shall be increased.... And he said, Go thy way, Daniel: for the words are closed up and sealed till the time of the end" (Dan. 12:4, 9).

At the same time in history, by turning to Revelation 22:10, John is told, "And he saith unto me, Seal not the sayings of the prophecy of this book: for the time is at hand." Therefore, we will study these two books together since both have to do with the time of the end.

Daniel 7—Vision of the Four Beasts

Now to explore Daniel's dream.

Daniel spake and said, I saw in my vision by night, and, behold, the four winds of the heaven strove upon the great sea. And four great beasts came up from the sea, diverse one from another. The first was like a lion, and had eagle's wings: I beheld till the wings thereof were plucked, and it was lifted up from the earth, and made to stand upon the feet as a man, and a man's heart was given to it. And behold another beast, a second, like to a bear, and it raised up itself on one side, and it had three ribs in the mouth of it between the teeth of it: and they said thus unto it, Arise, devour much flesh. After this I beheld, and lo another, like a leopard, which had upon the back of it four wings of a fowl; the beast had also four heads; and dominion was given to it.

After this I saw in the night visions, and behold a fourth beast, dreadful and terrible, and strong exceedingly; and it had great iron teeth: it devoured and brake in pieces, and stamped the residue with the feet of it: and it was diverse from all the beasts that were before it; and it had ten horns. I considered the horns, and, behold, there came up among them another little horn, before whom there were three of the first horns plucked up by the roots: and, behold, in this horn were eyes like the eyes of man, and a mouth speaking great things.

I beheld till the thrones were cast down, and the Ancient of days did sit, whose garment was white as snow, and the hair of his head like pure wool: his throne was like the fiery flame, and his wheels as burning fire. A fiery stream issued and came forth from before him: thousand thousands ministered unto him, and ten thousand time ten thousand stood before him: the judgment was set, and the books were opened. I beheld then because of the voice of the great words which the horn spake: I beheld even till the beast was slain, and his body destroyed, and given to the burning flame. As concerning the rest of the beasts, they had their dominion taken away: yet their lives were prolonged for a season and time. I saw in the night visions, and, behold, one like the Son of man came with the clouds of heaven, and came to the Ancient of days, and they brought him near before him. And there was given him dominion, and glory, and a kingdom, that all people, nations, and languages, should serve him: his dominion is an everlasting dominion, which shall not pass away, and his kingdom that which shall not be destroyed. (Dan. 7:2–14)

I came near unto one of them that stood by and asked him the truth of all this. So he told me, and made me to know the interpretation of the things. These great beasts, which are four, are four kings, which shall arise out of the earth. But the saints of the most High shall take the kingdom, and possess the kingdom for ever, even for ever and ever. Then I would know the truth of the fourth beast, which was diverse from all the others, exceeding dreadful, whose teeth were of iron, and his nails of brass; which devoured, brake in pieces, and stamped the residue with his feet; and of the ten horns that were in his head, and of the other which came up, and before whom three fell; even of that horn that had eyes, and a mouth that spake very great things, whose look was more stout than his fellows. I beheld, and the same horn made war with the saints, and prevailed against them; until the Ancient of days came, and judgment was given to the saints of the most High; and the time came that the saints possessed the kingdom. Thus he said, The fourth beast shall be the fourth kingdom upon earth, which shall be diverse from all kingdoms, and shall devour the whole earth, and shall tread it down, and break it in pieces. And the ten horns out of this kingdom are ten kings that shall arise: and another shall rise after them; and he shall be diverse from the first, and he shall subdue three kings. And he shall speak great words against the most High, and shall wear out the saints of the most High, and think to change times and laws: and they shall be given into his hands until a time and times and the dividing of time. But the judgment shall sit, and they shall take away his dominion, to consume and to destroy it unto the end. And the kingdom and dominion, and the greatness of the kingdom under the whole heaven, shall be given to the people of the saints of the most High, whose kingdom is an everlasting kingdom, and all dominions shall serve and obey him. Hitherto is the end of the matter. As for me Daniel, my cogitations much troubled me, and my countenance changed in me: but I kept the matter in my heart. (verses 16–28)

Let's do a little recapitulating here and see what kind of order we can put these facts into. Daniel was called to interpret King Nebuchadnezzar's dream as a young man. Now in his later years, he has a dream that, we are told again, represents the four universal kingdoms that will rule the earth. This didn't seem to bother Daniel, but what did concern him was the fourth kingdom that was divided into the ten horn kingdoms from which came a "little" horn. This little horn persecuted the saints for a period of time before the end of time. It spoke against God and His laws. Daniel is told that in the end the saints would overcome and possess the everlasting kingdom. He kept these things in his heart.

Daniel 8—More Details

It's now two years later, and Daniel is about to be told more details concerning his dream's interpretation. Daniel is at the palace in Shushan, in the province of Elam, when he has another vision.

Then I lifted up mine eyes, and saw, and, behold, there stood before the river [of Ulai] a ram which had two horns: and the two horns were high; but one was higher than the other, and the higher came up last. I saw the ram pushing westward, and northward, and southward; so that no beasts might stand before him, neither was there any that could deliver out of his hand; but he did according to his will, and became great. And as I was considering, behold, an he goat came from the west on the face of the whole earth, and touched not the ground: and the goat had a notable horn between his eyes. And he came to the ram that had two horns, which I had seen standing before the river, and ran unto him in the fury of his power. And I saw him come close unto the ram, and he was moved with choler against him, and smote the ram, and brake his two horns: and there was no power in the ram to stand before him, but he cast him down to the ground, and stamped upon him: and there was none that could deliver the ram out of his hand.

Therefore, the goat waxed very great: and when he was strong, the great horn was broken; and for it came up four notable ones toward the four winds of heaven. And out of one of them came forth a little horn, which waxed exceeding great, toward the south, and toward the east, and toward the pleasant land. And it waxed great, even to the host of heaven; and it cast down some of the host and of the stars to the ground, and stamped upon them. Yea, he magnified himself even to the prince of the host, and by him the daily sacrifice was taken away, and the place of the sanctuary was cast down. And an host was given him against the daily sacrifice by reason of transgression, and it cast down the truth to the ground; and it practiced, and prospered.

Then I heard one saint speaking, and another saint said unto that certain saint which spake, How long shall be the vision concerning the daily sacrifice, and the transgression of desolation, to give both the sanctuary and the host to be trodden under foot? And he said unto me, Unto two thousand and three hundred days; then shall the sanctuary be cleansed. And it came to pass, when I, even I Daniel, had seen the vision, and sought for the meaning, then, behold, there stood before me as the appearance of a man. And I heard a man's voice between the banks of Ulai, which called, and said, Gabriel, make this man to understand the vision.... And he said, Behold, I will make thee know what shall be in the last end of the indignation: for at the time appointed the end shall be.

The ram which thou sawest having two horns are the kings of Media and Persia. And the rough goat is the king of Grecia: and the great horn that is between his eyes is the first king. Now that being broken, whereas four stood up for it, four kingdoms shall stand up out of the nation, but not in his power. And in the latter time of their kingdom, when the transgressors are come to the full, a king of fierce countenance, and understanding dark sentences, shall stand up.... and he shall destroy wonderfully, and shall prosper, and practise, and shall destroy the mighty and the holy people. And through his policy also he shall cause craft to prosper in his hand; and he shall magnify himself in his heart, and by peace shall destroy many: he shall also stand up against the Prince of princes; but he shall be broken without hand. And the vision of the evening and the morning which was told is true: wherefore shut thou up the vision; for it shall be for many days. And I Daniel fainted, and was sick certain days ... and I was astonished at the vision, but none understood it. (Dan. 8:3–27)

In verse 27 Daniel wrote that after receiving the vision he "rose up, and did the king's business." Note that Daniel was handling King Belshazzar's business in the province of Elam at the palace in Shushan, and we find, in Esther 1:2, that was the palace of King Ahasuerus. We will see shortly that it was "Darius the son of Ahasuerus, of the seed of the Medes, which was made king over the realm of the Chaldeans" (Dan. 9:1).

End of Belshazzar's Reign— Hand Writing on the Wall

Before we explore chapter 9, let's return to Daniel 5 to close out King Belshazzar's reign and the end of Babylonian rule. We do not know how long his reign lasted, but we do know that the last night of his reign is recorded here. This is the account of a feast that turned tragic.

Belshazzar the king made a great feast to a thousand of his lords, and drank wine before the thousand. Belshazzar, whiles he tasted the wine, commanded to bring the golden and silver vessels which his father Nebuchadnezzar had taken out of the temple which was in Jerusalem; that the king, and his princes, his wives, and his concubines, might drink therein. Then they brought the golden vessels ... [and] drank in them. They drank wine, and praised the gods of gold, and of silver, and of brass, of iron, of wood, and of stone. In the same hour came forth fingers of a man's hand, and wrote over against the candlestick upon the plaister of the wall of the king's palace: and the king saw the part of the hand that wrote

Then the king's countenance was changed, and his thoughts troubled him, so that the joints of his loins were loosed, and his knees smote one against another. The king cried aloud to bring in the astrologers, the Chaldeans, and the soothsayers.... but they could not read the writing, nor make known to the king the interpretation thereof.... Now the queen ... spake and said, O king, live for ever: let not thy thoughts trouble thee ... There is a man in thy kingdom, in whom is the spirit of the holy gods; and in the days of thy father light and understanding and wisdom, like the wisdom of the gods, was found in him; whom the king Nebuchadnezzar thy father, the king, I say, thy father, made master of the magicians, astrologers, Chaldeans, and soothsayers; ...

Then was Daniel brought in before the king. And the king spake and said unto Daniel, Art thou that Daniel, which art of the children of the captivity of Judah, whom the king my father brought out of Jewry? I have even heard of thee, that the spirit of the gods is in thee, and that light and understanding and excellent wisdom is found in thee.... Now if thou canst read the writing, and make known to me the interpretation thereof, thou shalt be clothed with scarlet, and have a chain of gold about thy neck, and shalt be the third ruler in the kingdom.

Then Daniel answered and said before the king, Let thy gifts be to thyself, and give thy rewards to another; yet I will read the writing unto the king, and make known to him the interpretation. O thou king, the most high God gave Nebuchadnezzar thy father a kingdom, and majesty, and glory, and honour: And for the majesty that he gave him, all people, nations, and languages, trembled and feared before him: whom he would he slew; and whom he would he kept alive; and whom he would he set up, and whom he would he put down. But when his heart was lifted up, and his mind hardened in pride, he was deposed from his kingly throne, and they took his glory from him: And he was driven from the sons of men; and his heart was made like the beasts, and his dwelling was with the wild asses: they fed him with grass like oxen, and his body was wet with the dew of heaven; till he knew that the most high God ruled in the kingdom of men, and that he appointed over it whomsoever he will.

And thou his son, O Belshazzar, hast not humbled thine heart, though thou knewest all this; But hast lifted up thyself against the Lord of heaven; and they have brought the vessels of his house before thee, and thou, and thy lords, thy wives, and thy concubines, have drunk wine in them; and thou hast praised the gods of silver and gold, of brass, iron, wood, and stone, which see not, nor hear, nor know: and the God in whose hand thy breath is, and whose are all thy ways, hast thou not glorified: Then was the part of the hand sent from him; and this writing was written. And this is the writing that was written, Mene, Mene, Tekel, Upharsin.

This is the interpretation of the thing: Mene; God hath numbered thy kingdom, and finished it. Tekel; Thou art weighed in the balances, and art found wanting. Peres; Thy kingdom is divided, and given to the Medes and Persians.... In that night was Belshazzar the king of the Chaldeans slain. And Darius the Median took the kingdom, being about threescore and two years old [sixty-two years old]. (Dan. 5:1–31)

Did you notice that Belshazzar was fully aware of how God had dealt with his father's pride and Nebuchadnezzar's acknowledgement of God as the true God? James writes about the danger of not doing what we know is right: "Therefore to him that knoweth to do good, and doeth it not, to him it is sin" (James 4:17). It was with pride and arrogance that King Belshazzar deceived himself.

Darius had besieged the palace of Babylon, but it is said that Belshazzar had provisions enough to outlast those who besieged the walled city. However, there was a river that ran through the city with iron gates protecting those areas. While Belshazzar feasted and got drunk, Darius's army diverted the river and entered the city from beneath the gates. Our God works His will in mysterious ways, just as He does in protecting those who obey. Thus was Babylon defeated, and we see the fulfillment of Nebuchadnezzar's (gold head) kingdom giving way to the (silver chest) kingdom of the Medes and Persians; and Daniel's ram to the he goat. God speaks and it comes to pass.

Medes Rule—Daniel Learns More About the Future of God's People

Is there a connection between Daniel's being in Shushan and receiving the vision of the ram and the goat? Was Darius privy to that vision and also to the handwriting on the wall as a factor in his decision to make Daniel first of the three presidents over all the kingdom? We can only speculate since we have no clear "thus saith the Lord," and no matter, this isn't about who's who but, it is about realizing that our God is in charge and His will is fulfilled in our lives and world events.

Now let's return to those things with which Daniel was perplexed. The Medes and the Persians are now in control of the world's kingdoms. Daniel is concerned about what will happen to God's chosen people and the sanctuary, God's dwelling place on earth. He knows God is in charge; therefore, he searches the prophetic writings to see if he can find some answers to these things he has been privileged to be shown. Daniel knows, as do the other prophets, the writings of Amos: "Surely the Lord God will do nothing, but he revealeth his secret unto his servants the prophets." Daniel then writes in chapter 9, verse 2, "In the first year of his [Darius] reign I Daniel understood by books the numbers of the years, whereof the word of the Lord came to Jeremiah the prophet, that he would accomplish seventy years in the desolations of Jerusalem" (see also 2 Chron. 36:21; Ezra 1:1; Jer. 25:11, 12).

Daniel's intercessory prayer for Israel and its captivity is recorded in chapter 9, verses 3–19. In verses 20 and 21 we find the following, "And whiles I was speaking, and praying, and confessing my sin and the sin of my people Israel, and presenting my supplication before the Lord my God for the holy mountain of my God; Yea, whiles I was speaking in prayer, even the man Gabriel, whom I had seen in the vision at the beginning, being caused to fly swiftly, touched me about the time of the evening oblation."

Gabriel is sent again to clarify some of the things that troubled Daniel concerning the vision of the ram and the goat, in regards to the people of God and the sanctuary. The vision had been shut up until the end. Therefore, we continue with Gabriel speaking to Daniel:

> And he informed me, and talked with me, and said, O Daniel, I am now come forth to give thee skill and understanding. At the beginning of thy supplications the commandment came forth, and I am come to shew thee; for thou art greatly beloved: therefore understand the matter, and consider the vision. Seventy weeks are determined upon thy people and upon thy holy city, to finish the transgression, and to make an end of sins, and to make reconciliation for iniquity, and to bring in everlasting righteousness, and to seal up the vision and prophecy, and to anoint the most Holy. Know therefore and understand, that from the going forth of the commandment to restore and to build Jerusalem unto the Messiah the Prince shall be seven weeks, and threescore and two weeks: the street shall be built again, and the wall, even in troublous times. And after threescore and two weeks shall Messiah be cut off, but not for himself: and the people of the prince that shall come shall destroy the city and the sanctuary; and the end thereof shall be with a flood, and unto the end of the war desolations are determined. And he shall confirm the covenant with many for one week: and in the midst of the week he shall cause the sacrifice and the oblation to cease, and for the overspreading of abominations he shall make it desolate, even until the consummation, and that determined shall be poured upon the desolate. (verses 22–27)

At this point, let's review and understand what Gabriel has been revealing to Daniel in these dreams and visions. We will begin by comparing Daniel's closed book—"shut up the words, and seal the book, even to the time of the end" (Dan. 12:4)—with John's open book—"And he saith unto me, Seal not the sayings of the prophecy of this book: for the time is at hand" (Rev. 22:10).

We have been getting glimpses of how God protected His people throughout the past ages in these historical events, and it was predicted that evil men and nations would continue to "the end." We also know the mastermind behind their evil deeds. This drama of obedience with love and peace, as contrasted with Satan's plan of selfishness, self-rule, no laws, and strife, has to continue to the point where no one can doubt that God's way is the only way to govern the universe. In the process of obtaining that necessary spiritual-minded goal, it is necessary for us to realize what the ultimate results of this internal conflict will bring. It isn't without purpose that events shape our lives, and how the twig is bent determines how the tree will grow. We know that we shall die, but what then? The following pages will answer that question.

In all these visions and dreams, Daniel was concerned with the ultimate outcome for God's chosen people. He is fully aware of God's promises and His leading among the people; he is also fully aware of the people's failures to be obedient by following after other gods.

All these visions center around wars and conflicts that occurred as the result of setting up and tearing down kingdoms here on earth, revealing that God is in charge of our lives. The end features the restoration of God's eternal kingdom.

In chapter 8, verse 13 Daniel asks this question, "How long shall be the vision concerning the daily sacrifice, and the transgression of desolation, to give both the sanctuary and the host to be trodden under foot?" The response comes in verse 14: ""Unto two thousand and three hundred days; then shall the sanctuary be cleansed." It is to this question and answer that Gabriel is sent to Daniel to "understand the matter, and consider the vision" (Dan. 9:23) We find more information in verses 24 and 25: "Seventy weeks are determined upon thy people ... Know therefore and understand, that from the going forth of the commandment to restore and to build Jerusalem unto the Messiah the Prince shall be seven weeks, and threescore and two weeks [sixty-nine weeks]." Do we know when this decree was given? Yes, the answer is found in Ezra 6:14 and 7:11–28, which is the year 457 BC.

Notice the following verses: "After the number of the days in which ye searched the land, even forty days, each day for a year, shall ye bear your iniquities, even forty years, and ye shall know my breach of promise" (Num. 14:34). "And thou shall bear the iniquity of the house of Judah forty days: I have appointed thee each day for a year" (Ezek. 4:6). Therefore, the 2300 days would be 2300 prophetic years, and the seventy weeks equals 490 days, which translates to 490 years, beginning in 457 BC. The seven weeks (forty-nine years) to rebuild Jerusalem ended in 408 BC when the city and temple were completed. Sixty-two more weeks (434 years) reached to the Messiah or Christ. This is a total of sixty-nine weeks (483 years) from the autumn of 457 BC to the autumn of AD 27, which is the year that Christ was anointed by the Holy Ghost at His baptism, when the voice of God said, "This is my beloved Son, in whom I am well pleased" (Matt. 3:17; see also verses 13–16 and Acts 10:38). Christ began His reconciliatory work at this time, the seventieth week, and confirmed the covenant with many during that week, but was in the midst of the week "cut off." Thus, the prophecy was fulfilled—the Lamb was slain from the foundation of the earth. The last half of that seventieth week (three and a half years) occurred in AD 34 when Jesus was crucified, Stephen is stoned, and the leaders of Israel are in full rebellion to rid the nation of the followers of "the way." It marks the official rejection of Christ as the Messiah and the end of the seventy-weeks (490 years) prophecy.

The following verses document the rejection that the Messiah experienced among His own people:

O Jerusalem, Jerusalem, thou that killest the prophets, and stonest them which are sent unto thee, how often would I have gathered thy children together, even as a hen gathereth her chickens under her wings, and ye would not! Behold, your house is left unto you desolate. (Matt. 23:37, 38)

But Esaias is very bold, and saith, [Isa. 65:1] I was found of them that sought me not; I was made manifest into them that asked not after me. But to Israel he saith, All day long I have stretched forth my hands unto a disobedient and gainsaying people. (Rom. 10:20, 21)

I say then, Hath God cast away his people? God forbid. For I also am an Israelite, of the seed of Abraham, of the tribe of Benjamin. God hath not cast away his people which he foreknew. Wot ye not what the scriptures saith of Elias?... Lord, they have killed thy prophets, and digged down thine altars; and I am left alone, and they seek my life. But what saith the answer of God unto him? I have reserved to myself seven thousand men, who have not bowed the knee to the image of Baal. Even so then at this present time also there is a remnant according to the election of grace....

And if some of the branches be broken off, and thou, being a wild olive tree, wert grafted in among them, and with them partakest of the root and fatness of the olive tree; ... because of unbelief they were broken off, and thou standest by faith. Be not highminded, but fear: For if God spared not the natural branches, take heed lest he also spare not thee. Behold therefore the goodness and severity of God: on them which fell, severity; but toward thee, goodness, if thou continue in his goodness: otherwise thou also shalt be cut off. And they also, if they abide not still in unbelief, shall be grafted in: for God is able to graft them in again.... And so all Israel shall be saved: as it is written, There shall come out of Sion the Deliverer, and shall turn away ungodliness from Jacob: ... For God hath concluded them all in unbelief, that he might have mercy upon all. (Rom. 11:1–5, 17–32)

It is clear from these scriptures that God works in and through His people who remain faithful to His principles and will. We all partake of the root and fatness of the olive tree, which is symbolic of Christ Jesus. It is also clear that the nation of Israel is no longer representative of God's chosen people. No nation has that distinction today. God has adherents in all nations.

There was a remnant of the nation of Israel who represented the branches that were not broken off—these were the apostles and those of Israel who stopped following the false leaders of Israel to follow the correct and true teaching of the apostles as given to them by Jesus. There were also the Gentiles who were now believers, and these were represented as the "wild" branches that were grafted into the true tree. These "wild" branches didn't make a new tree or religious philosophy, but they continued in the apostle's doctrines—God's true principles. These were "followers" of the way. They were called Christians because they followed Christ's teachings. He remains the same yesterday, today, and forever. His principles are from everlasting to everlasting.

Cleansing of the Sanctuary

Let's pick up the 2300-day/year prophecy where we left off. The seventy weeks were cut off of the 2300 days/years—2300 minus 490 equals 1810 years. When we add these 1810 years to AD 34, we come to AD 1844. It was in this year that the sanctuary would be cleansed.

What is the significance of the sanctuary? To learn about this we must go back to heaven. "And the Lord spake unto Moses, saying, … And let them make me a sanctuary; that I may dwell among them. According to all that I shew thee, after the pattern of the tabernacle…. And look that thou make them after their pattern, which was shewed thee in the mount" (Exod. 25:1, 8, 9, 40). "Now of the things which we have spoken this is the sum: We have such an high priest, who is set on the right hand of the throne of the Majesty in the heavens; a minister of the sanctuary, and of the true tabernacle, which the Lord pitched, and not men" (Heb. 8:1, 2).

What is the function of the sanctuary? Why was it necessary for the earthly sanctuary to be patterned after the heavenly? The sanctuary is not just a place for men to meet with God or for God to dwell with men. It has to do with mankind being made right with God. Nothing that defiles can come into the presence of a holy God and live, and that means anything in heaven, the universe, or earth. Remember, we have seen several times that Christ is "the Lamb slain from the foundation of the world" (Rev. 13:8). It is important that the services performed in the sanctuary and their meaning be clearly understood, and the necessity for these services is seen in the light of God's redemptive plan.

First, let's examine portions of the sanctuary design, its services, and their significance. The sanctuary consisted of two compartments—the Holy Place and the Most Holy Place. These were surrounded by a walled rectangular courtyard. Near the "door" was the altar of sacrifice. We will not go into the various other items of the courtyard or the compartments and their functions in this study.

A sinner would bring his sacrifice to the door of the sanctuary. He would confess his sins while placing his hand upon the head of the animal, thereby transferring his guilt to the animal. Then he would kill the animal by cutting its throat. The priest would take some of the blood and place it on the horns of the altar and sprinkle it before the veil of the sanctuary as an atonement for present sins. (There were various other sacrifices as well.)

The "cleansing of the sanctuary" had to do with the annual feast representing the judgment day and the eradicating of sin/wickedness/evil from the world. It was an annual memorial that focused on the repentance of sins and the second coming of our Lord when all things will be restored and made new.

The second compartment, the Most Holy Place, contained the ark of God with the mercy seat. The ark contained the tablets of stone on which were written the Ten Commandments, manna, and Aaron's rod that had budded. The ark symbolized God's righteous judgment and mercy. The Most Holy Place was only entered on the last day of the year, the Day of Atonement. On that day the sanctuary was cleansed, which represented the end of the world when all sin will be eradicated (cleansed) from all of God's creation. Our High Priest's blood will cleanse the heavenly sanctuary of the evils of all sin.

This annual day is also a symbolic judgment day because those whose sins were not transferred were "cut off" from the congregation (see Lev. 16:5–34; 23:27–33). Those whose sins were transferred to the sanctuary were forgiven. "But into the second went the high priest alone once every year, not without blood, which he offered for himself, and for the errors of the people" (Heb. 9:7). On the Day of Atonement two goats were selected, one for the sacrifice, the other as the scapegoat (see Lev. 16:5, 8, 15, 16, 20–22). The Lord's goat represented Jesus, whose blood cleanses from sin: "But with the precious blood of Christ, as of a lamb without blemish and without spot" (1 Peter 1:19; see also Acts 8:32; Rev. 6:16). This offering cleansed the sanctuary, and the sins of the people were atoned for.

The scapegoat symbolized Satan, the great tempter and originator of all sin. The scapegoat was brought to the door of the sanctuary, and all the sins Satan tempted God's people to commit, which were repented of, were placed on his head. He was then led away into a land "not inhabited" (Lev. 16:22). (During the millennium, the earth will "not be inhabited.") Christ is our High Priest in the heavenly sanctuary. "It was therefore necessary that the patterns of things in the heavens should be purified with these; but the heavenly things themselves with better sacrifices than these" (Heb. 9:23). The earthly sanctuary was a figure of that time (verse 9). Christ is the minister of the heavenly sanctuary (Heb. 8:2), and He offers His own blood to cleanse us (Heb. 9:23; see also Eph. 5:2).

Please note: Christ's work as our High Priest in heaven could not begin until after He offered Himself as an atoning gift for our sins on the cross. He ascended into heaven as our mediator and High Priest in the heavenly places (Heb. 9:25, 26). His work in the cleansing of the heavenly sanctuary could not begin until the end of the 2300 days/years, which came about in 1844 (see Dan. 8:14). At the close of the work of the ancient high priest on the Day of Atonement, he put off his robes and came forth and blessed the assembled people who had gathered around the sanctuary (Lev. 16:21–24). So, when our Savior finishes His work as our mediator in heaven, He will appear with glory at His second coming to bless us with immortality and take us to heaven. At the same time, the great antitypical scapegoat, Satan, will bear his responsibility for his part in the sins of God's people in an uninhabited land, and at the end of the thousand years, Satan, his evil angels, and all the wicked will be destroyed in the lake of fire. "So Christ was once offered to bear the sins of many; and unto them that look for him shall he appear the second time without sin unto salvation" (Heb. 9:28). The righteous will be with Christ in heaven and then in the new earth.

These texts make it clear that Christ is mediating our case before the throne of God today. He is in the process of cleansing the sanctuary. This is the judgment phase. It has to do with God's book of life that is mentioned in Daniel 7: "And the Ancient of days did sit ... the judgment was set, and the books were opened" (verses 9, 10). Moses said, "Yet now, if thou wilt forgive their sin—; and if not, blot me, I pray thee, out of thy book which thou hast written. And the Lord said unto Moses, Whosoever hath sinned against me, him will I blot out of my book" (Exod. 32:32, 33; see also Ps. 69:28; Dan. 12:1; Luke 10:20; Rev. 3; 13:8; 20:12).

Some may wonder who will be judged during the judgment. The Bible says that "the time is come that judgment must begin at the house of God: and if it first begin at us, what shall the end be of them that obey not the gospel of God?" (1 Peter 4:17)

When Christ has finished His work of mediation in the sanctuary and has cleaned it, then He will "stand up, the great prince which standeth for the children of thy people: and there shall be a time of trouble, such as never was since there was a nation even to that same time: and at that time thy people shall be delivered, every one that shall be found written in the books" (Dan. 12:1). "He that is unjust, let him be unjust still: and he which is filthy, let him be filthy still: and he that is righteous, let him be righteous still: and he that is holy, let him be holy still. And, behold, I come quickly; and my reward is with me, to give every man according as his work shall be" (Rev. 22:11, 12).

Let's take note of some other things about the sanctuary and its services before leaving this subject. At the moment that Christ died, it was time for the evening sacrifice. "And it was about the sixth hour, and there was darkness over all the earth until the ninth hour. And the sun was darkened, and the veil of the temple was rent in the midst" (Luke 23:44, 45). When the veil was "rent in twain from the top to the bottom," it signified that we can now come directly to God through the blood of Jesus, our mediator and advocate. "And when Jesus had cried with a loud voice, he said, Father, into thy hands I commend my spirit: and having said thus, he gave up the ghost" (Luke 23:46).

The book of Hebrews contains a passage that details the importance of Christ's sacrifice and the cleansing that is offered through His blood:

> And almost all things are by the law purged with blood; and without shedding of blood is no remission. It was therefore necessary that the patterns of things in the heavens should be purified with these; but the heavenly things themselves with better sacrifices than these. For Christ is not entered into the holy places made with hands, which are the figures of the true; but into heaven itself, now to appear in the presence of God for us: Nor yet that he should offer himself often, as the high priest entereth into the holy place every year with blood of others; For then must he often have suffered since the foundation of the world: but now once in the end of the world hath he appeared to put away sin by the sacrifice of himself. And as it is appointed unto men once to die, but after this the judgment: So Christ was once offered to bear the sins of many; and unto them that look for him shall he appear the second time without sin unto salvation. (Heb. 9:22–28)

Paul writes in Colossians 2:14–22:

> Blotting out the handwriting of the ordinances that was against us, which was contrary to us, and took it out of the way, nailing it to his cross; And having spoiled principalities and powers, he made a shew of them openly, triumphing over them in it. Let no man therefore judge you in meat, or in drink, or in respect of an holyday, or of the new moon, or of the sabbath days: Which are a shadow of things to come; but the body is of Christ. Let no man beguile you of your reward in a voluntary humility and worshipping of angels, intruding into those things which he hath not seen, vainly puffed up by his fleshly mind, and not holding the Head, from which all the body by joints and bands having nourishment ministered, and knit together, increaseth with the increase of God. Wherefore if ye be dead with Christ from the rudiments of the world, why, as though living in the world, are ye subject to ordinances, (Touch not; taste not; handle not; which all are to perish with the using;) after the commandments and doctrines of men? Which things have indeed a shew of wisdom in

will worship, and humility, and neglecting of the body: not in any honour to the satisfying of the flesh. (Col. 2:14–23)

Type met antitype when Christ died on the cross. The sacrificial ordinances and ceremonies and rituals that took place in the sanctuary all pointed to Christ. Therefore, they were fulfilled with His death. The daily sacrifices, the Passover, the Day of Atonement, the meat and drink offerings, etc., were the things that were "nailed to the cross" and came to an end with Christ's overwhelmingly sufficient sacrifice. They were "a shadow of things to come." Victory is secure for all those who choose to accept God's gracious, free gift of life by faith and unconditionally surrender to the obedience of His will. Soon "time will be no more."

With the tearing of the sanctuary veil "from top to bottom" at Christ's death and the destruction of the temple in AD 70, what form did worship take? Did God's followers have to come to the temple to worship, or was there another way for them to connect with God?

What? know ye not that your body is the temple of the Holy Ghost which is in you, which ye have of God, and ye are not your own? For ye are bought with a price: therefore glorify God in your body, and in your spirit, which are God's. (1 Cor. 6:19, 20).

For ye are the temple of the living God; as God hath said, I will dwell in them, and walk in them; and I will be their God, and they shall be my people. (2 Cor. 6:16; see also Lev. 26:12)

Ye also ... are built up a spiritual house, an holy priesthood, to offer up spiritual sacrifices, acceptable to God by Jesus Christ. (1 Peter 2:5)

For this is the covenant that I will make with the house of Israel after those days, saith the Lord; I will put my laws into their mind, and write them in their hearts: and I will be to them a God, and they shall be to me a people. (Heb. 8:10; see also Jer. 31:33; Ezek. 11:19)

Salvation is an individual matter that each person must work out with God (see Ezek. 14:14). No one will be allowed in heaven just because they belonged to a certain nation, tribe, ethnic group, family, or church. Salvation is obtained by believing in God and having the indwelling of the Holy Spirit in one's life. We must model the character of Christ Jesus, for He displayed God's perfect love based on His relationship with God the Father. However, just because we have a close relationship with Jesus doesn't mean that we should not fellowship with like believers or try to "go it alone." We are admonished in Hebrews 10:25 to not forsake "the assembling of ourselves together, as the manner of some is; but exhorting one another: and so much the more, as ye see the day approaching." The early believers met in the synagogues until they were forced out because of persecution. Then they met in believers' homes or anywhere that they found sympathy.

We have discovered in our study of Daniel that there were four world kingdoms and a fifth kingdom that would last forever, that is, God's kingdom. Daniel's prophecy revealed the cleansing of the sanctuary and the judgment. We also learned that Daniel's prophecy was to be "shut up" until the time of the end. In contrast we found that the book of Revelation is an open book and has to do with the "time of the end," which we will now study.

Chapter 7
Knowledge and Understanding From the Revelation of Jesus

John's Revelation and Things to Come

We will find that the symbolism and interpretations given to Daniel will be meaningful in Revelation and that Revelation will fill in details just as the later dreams of Daniel added more information to what was initially given. We also saw the same format in Genesis with the accounts of creation and the other historic recorded events. We will be looking at the similarities of events, times, and circumstances of both books rather than chapter by chapter. That way we will be able to see the full picture and true facts.

First, a little history regarding the writing of Revelation. This is not the Revelation of John, but the Revelation given to John by Jesus Christ "to shew unto his servants things which must shortly come to pass" (Rev. 1:1). John was in exile on the Isle of Patmos because of religious persecution when he wrote this book around AD 100. The book was written to strengthen God's people wherever they were, for they had been scattered due to persecution. It was also to serve as a reminder to them, like Daniel, that God is still in charge. It also gives readers a glimpse into heaven and into the new earth.

Verse 2 and 3 state, "Who bare record of the word of God, and of the testimony of Jesus Christ, and of all things that he saw. Blessed is he that readeth, and they that hear the words of this prophecy, and keep those things which are written therein: for the time is at hand."

John begins to unfold to us what he saw in the next few verses: "John to the seven churches which are in Asia: Grace be unto you, and peace, from him which is, and which was, and which is to come; and from the seven Spirits which are before his throne; and from Jesus Christ, who is the faithful witness, and the first begotten of the dead, and the prince of the king of the earth. Unto him that loved us, and washed us from our sins in his own blood, and hath made us kings and priests unto God and his Father; to him be glory and dominion for ever and ever. Amen" (verses 4–6).

Notice Jesus' testimony in John 12:49, "For I have not spoken of myself; but the Father which sent me, he gave me a commandment, what I should say, and what I should speak," Let's also read Revelation 22:16: "I Jesus have sent mine angel to testify unto you these things in the churches. I am the root and offspring of David, and the bright and morning star."

There can be no doubt about it. This is a message from the triune God and is to be a revelation of events that will occur in the world and will impact His people down through the ages until the coming of Christ when the earth will be made new and all things that were marred by disobedience will be restores. Let's continue reading from Revelation 1:

> Behold, he cometh with clouds; and every eye shall see him, and they also which pierced him: and all kindreds of the earth shall wail because of him. Even so, Amen. I am Alpha and Omega, the beginning and the ending, saith the Lord, which is, and which was, and which is to come, the Almighty…. I was in the Spirit on the Lord's day, and heard behind me a great voice, as of a trumpet, saying, I am Alpha and Omega, the first and the last: and, What thou seest, write in a book, and send it unto the seven churches which are in Asia; unto Ephesus, and unto Smyrna, and unto Pergamos, and unto Thyatira, and unto Sardis, and unto Philadelphia, and unto Laodicea. (verses 7–11)

Please note, it was not John who selected the churches to whom these letters or book were to be sent. These churches were selected by Jesus for a purpose, which we shall see.

> And I turned to see the voice that spake to me. And being turned, I saw seven golden candlesticks; and in the midst of the seven candlesticks one like unto the Son of man, clothed with a garment down to the foot, and girt about the paps with a golden girdle. His head and his hairs were white like wool, as white as snow; and his eyes were as a flame of fire; and his feet like unto fine brass, as if they burned in a furnace; and his voice as the sound of many waters. And he had in his right hand seven stars … and his countenance was as the sun shineth in his strength. And when I saw him, I fell at his feet as dead. And he laid his right hand upon me, saying unto me, Fear not; I am the first and the last: I am he that liveth, and was dead; and behold, I am alive for evermore, Amen; and have the keys of hell and of death. Write the things which thou hast seen, and the things which are, and the things which shall be hereafter; the mystery of the seven stars which thou sawest in my right hand, and the seven golden candlesticks. The seven stars are the angels of the seven churches: and the seven candlesticks which thou sawest are the seven churches. (verses 12–20)

In Scripture the numbers seven and twelve are symbolic of completeness, which is evident in the seven seals, the seven trumpets, the seven last plagues, and in this case, the complete church age from the apostolic church to the last church age at Christ's coming.

Just as Daniel prophesied that there would be four world kingdoms—and as you will remember, God's people would be trampled upon for a times, a time and a dividing of time (Dan. 7:25; 8:10; Rev. 12:14), we find how God's people fared during these end-time predicted events. As we study the letters written to the seven churches, let us remember that they are both literal and figurative or symbolic of the conditions the church finds itself in from the time of the apostles to the church that will be present when Christ returns. Also, the church is the group of individuals who comprise the assembly of God's people. Individually we are the church, whether it is two or three persons or thousands (see Matt. 18:20).

The Seven Churches—Symbolism

God chose the churches and placed them in the order that would match the spiritual conditions of the church for that church age. Interpretation of a scriptural passage will be dealt with as we come to each new thing. If the context denotes a literal interpretation, that is the meaning that will be applied, and if it also could have a symbolic interpretation, that will be considered and applied. The Bible is its own best interpreter. Dreams and visions are symbolic.

Read Revelation 2 and 3 to get an overview of the entire message given to John and addressed to the churches. Remember that John is exiled to the Isle of Patmos because of his preaching and teaching the word of God and having the testimony of Jesus Christ. We can only imagine that nothing could leave the island unless it was first approved to leave by those in charge. John well knew of Daniel's writings and the symbolism used therein and so would his readers, but his guards would have only shaken their heads at the strange babblings of a demented old man writing to the churches.

The church of Ephesus means "desirable" and represents the condition of the church in the Apostolic Age from Christ to AD 100. The commendation is "I know thy works, and thy labour, and they patience, and how thou canst not bear them which are evil: and thou hast tried them which say they are apostles, and are not, and hast found them liars" (Rev. 2:2). They labored, had patience in Jesus' name and did not grow weary (verse 3). False teachers, preachers, and doctrines came into the church, but the church tested them to see whom they could trust (see Matt. 24:11, 24; 2 Peter 2:1; 1 John 4:1; 1 Tim. 6:20). Yet God condemned them because they had "forsaken the love you had at first…. Repent and do the things you did at first. If you do not repent, I will come to you and remove your lampstand [the Source of Light] from its place. But you have this in your favor: You hate the practices of the Nicolaitans, which I also hate. Whoever has ears, let them hear what the Spirit says to the churches. To the one who is victorious, I will give the right to eat from the tree of life" (Rev. 2:4–7, NIV). There has always been a remnant that has and will follow God and overcome.

These conditions that happened to and were seen in the church in Ephesus are representative of our individual lives. Initially we have a zeal for God and His ways, but, if allowed, God is gradually pushed out for things of this world. However, all is not lost if we repent.

The church of Smyrna (from AD 100–323) means "myrrh" or perfume and represents the period of the church during the initial persecution from the apostles to the conversion of Constantine when the empire became Christian and pagan persecution largely ceased. Verse 10 says, "I tell you, the devil will put some of you in prison to test you, and you will suffer persecution for ten days." Remember the year for a day principle in prophecy. The ten years of pagan persecution was under Diocletian (AD 303–313).

The church of Pergamos (AD 313–538) means "height" or "elevation" and portrays the conditions of the church from the time of Constantine to the beginning of the 1260 years of tribulation. "Nevertheless, I have a few things against you: There are some among you who hold to the teaching of Balaam, who taught Balak to entice the Israelites to sin so that they ate food sacrificed to idols and committed sexual immorality. Likewise, you also have those who hold to the teaching of the Nicolatians. Repent therefore! Otherwise, I will soon come to you and will fight against them with the sword of my mouth.... To the one who is victorious, I will give some of the hidden manna" (Rev. 2:14–17, NIV).

The church of Thyatira (AD 538–1798) means "contrition" or "song of labor." John wrote, "I know your deeds, your love and faith, your service and perseverance, and that you are now doing more than you did at first. Nevertheless, I have this against you: You tolerate that woman Jezebel, who calls herself a prophet. By her teaching she misleads my servants into sexual immorality and the eating food sacrificed to idols. I have given her time to repent of her immorality, but she is unwilling.... I will repay each of you according to your deeds. Now ... to you who do not hold to her teachings and have not learned Satan's so-called deep secrets, 'I will not impose any other burden on you, except to hold on to what you have until I come.' To the one who is victorious and does my will to the end, I will give authority over the nations" (verses 20–26, NIV).

The church of Sardis (1798–1833) means "that which remains" and symbolizes God's true people of the reformation times. "I know your deeds; you have a reputation of being alive, but you are dead. Wake up! Strengthen what remains and is about to die, for I have found your deeds unfinished in the sight of my God. Remember, therefore, what you have received and heard; hold it fast, and repent. But if you do not wake up, I will come like a thief, and you will not know at what time I will come to you. Yet you have a few people in Sardis who have not soiled their clothes. They will walk with me, dressed in white, for they are worthy. The one who is victorious will, like them, be dressed in white" (Rev. 3:1–5, NIV).

The church of Philadelphia (1833–1844) means "brotherly love" and represents the church during the great Advent movement. It was during this period that a great awakening of interest in the promised second coming of Christ occurred simultaneously in the "Christian churches" of the world. The imminent return of our Lord was the focus of this interdenominational worldwide group. Among these were Methodists, Baptists, Episcopalians, Congregationalists, and others.

The most prominent preacher in this movement in the United States was a Baptist minister named William Miller, and the movement took on his name and became known as the "Millerites." He was assisted by a traveling Methodist minister named Fredrich Wheeler who helped to establish and propagate the advent message and the soon return of the Lord. This led to the great disappointment when the Lord did not come as thought in October of 1844.

However, the disappointment resulted in the founding of the Seventh-day Adventist Church a few years later. Mrs. Rachel Oakes (later Preston), a Seventh Day Baptist, presented the truth concerning the seventh-day Sabbath to this remnant body of seekers, thus completing the name of the church. This was the great awakening of God's children, and we will see how all this unfolds according to God's hand in this book of revelations.

At this time attention is drawn to Christ's work as our High Priest in the heavenly sanctuary. "I know your deeds. See, I have placed before you an open door that no one can shut. I know that you have little strength, yet you have kept my word and have not denied my name.... Since you have kept my command to endure patiently, I will also keep you from the hour of trial that is going to come upon the whole world to test the inhabitants of the earth. I am coming soon. Hold on to what you have ... The one who is victorious I will make a pillar in the temple of my God" (verses 8–12, NIV).

The church of Laodicea (1844–to the end) means "judging the people." "I know your deeds, that you are neither cold nor hot. I wish you were either one or the other! So, because you are lukewarm—neither hot nor cold—I am about to spit you out of my mouth. You say, 'I am rich; I have acquired wealth and do not need a thing.' But you do not realize that you are wretched, pitiful, poor, blind and naked. I counsel you to buy from me gold refined in the fire, so you can become rich; and white clothes to wear, so you can cover your shameful nakedness, and salve to put on your eyes, so you can see. Those whom I love I rebuke and discipline. So be earnest, and repent.... To the one who is victorious, I will give the right to sit with me on my throne" (verses 15–21, NIV).

If we turn back to Daniel 7:10–14, we read that "the judgment was set, and the books were opened." Judgment will begin with the house of God and those who profess to be His children. As previously mentioned, these stages or ages of the church could also represent the spiritual condition of our individual lives, so there is a dual application. As new worshippers of God, we find ourselves like a newlywed, wanting to please our spouse. Then the honeymoon fades, and we begin to slip away from correct principles. We may be in any of the stages as represented by the churches, but please note, the Lord is always holding out His arms ready to reclaim us from our foolish and sometimes stubborn selves. He only instructs us to "repent, and turn yourselves from all your transgressions; so iniquity shall not be your ruin" (Ezek. 18:30). His invitation to us of this Laodicean age is found in Revelation 3:20: "I stand at the door, and knock: if any man hear my voice, and open the door, I will come in to him."

This is the message that God has been giving to all generations of mankind: My self-sacrificing love is the only rule for "life." I am the Lamb slain from the foundation of the world. "Him that cometh to me I will in no wise cast out" (John 6:37). Christ says, Be one with Me as I am one with the Father (see John 17:11; 1 John 1:3).

In Daniel there was an emphasis on God and His being in control of nations and events with the people of God shown in the background. Here in Revelation we find the reverse is true. What is happening to God's people during these periods of church history is paramount, and the kingdoms are the structure in time phases just as we speak of the Dark Ages, the Revolutionary Age, the Age of Enlightenment, and the Industrial Age. This present age could be called the age of advanced knowledge in technology and travel. Daniel was told to "shut up the words, and seal the book, even to the time of the end: many shall run to and fro, and knowledge shall be increased" (Dan. 12:4).

Think about that statement in light of how we operate today! We trade with people all over the earth, and it doesn't take years or months. A cargo plane could fly around the earth and stop at multiple countries to unload and load goods and be back at its home base in seven days with ease. We can connect to the World Wide Web by computer and access knowledge in every major library around the world. The advances in medicine have added years to our lives. All of this is good. However, Satan still entices humans through his principles of destruction, greed, lust, pride, and the desire to be like the Most High. He also misuses good things to destroy mankind. We call it man's inhumanity to man. The nations of the world have weapons of mass destruction that are used against other nations, and terrorists use them against society, not for the good of people, but for the suppression and oppression of right principles in most cases. We will explore this more when we study Revelation 12–14.

The Twenty-four Elders and Four Beasts

Revelation 4 and 5 contains several verses that we will study in more detail than the other verses. Just after being shown the seven churches and while still in vision, John was briefly invited through an open door in heaven. "Come up hither, and I will shew thee things which must be hereafter" (Rev. 4:1). John found himself in the throne room of God the Father, which is surrounded by the seats of twenty-four elders. From their white raiment and crowns of gold, which are the tokens of overcomers in the warfare against Satan, we know that these once walked the same earth as all God's people.

Matthew records the resurrection of some of the saints at Christ's resurrection (Matt. 27:52, 53); Paul records their ascension to heaven (Eph. 4:8); and John beholds them in heaven performing the sacred duties that they were raised up to accomplish. Now these were giving glory, honor, and thanks to God and saying, "Thou art worthy, O Lord, to receive glory and honour, and power: for thou hast created all things, and for thy pleasure they are and were created" (Rev. 4:11).

John also saw four beasts in the midst of the throne and round about the throne, which he described as having six wings and full of eyes before and behind. One was like a lion, another like a calf, the third with a face like a man, and the last like an eagle. "And they rest not day and night, saying, Holy, holy, holy, Lord God Almighty, which was, and is, and is to come" (verse 8). These are felt to be from the same group of redeemed that the twenty-four elders came from; however, I wonder if it would be stretching things to suggest that these four are the representatives of the initial creation of God: the beast of the earth, the cattle, man, and the fowl were all created good.

> For the earnest expectation of the creature waiteth for the manifestation of the sons of God. For the creature was made subject to the vanity, not willingly, but by reason of him who hath subjected the same in hope, because the creature itself also shall be delivered from the bondage of corruption into the glorious liberty of the children of God. For we know that the whole creation groaneth and travaileth in pain together until now. And not only they, but ourselves also, which have the firstfruits of the Spirit, even we ourselves groan within ourselves, waiting for the adoption, to wit, the redemption of our body. (Rom. 8:19–23)

Could Enoch be the representative of the human race?

The Seven Seals

We find a continuation of this scene in Revelation 5 with the Father holding a sealed book in His right hand that seemingly no one is worthy of opening. "And one of the elders saith unto me, Weep not: behold, the Lion of the tribe of Judah, the Root of David, hath prevailed to open the book, and to loose the seven seals thereof. And I beheld, and, lo, in the midst of the throne and of the four beasts, and in the midst of the elders, stood a Lamb as it had been slain, having seven horns and seven eyes, which are the seven Spirits of God sent forth into all the earth" (Rev. 5:5, 6).

Continuing a few verses later, we read, "And they sung a new song, saying, Thou art worthy to take the book, and to open the seals thereof: for thou wast slain, and hast redeemed us to God by thy blood out of every kindred, and tongue, and people, and nation; and hast made us unto our God kings and priests: and we shall reign on the earth" (verses 9, 10).

It was the Lamb slain from the foundation of the world that was worthy to open the book with seven seals which was in the Father's right hand. "And every creature which is in heaven, and on the earth, and under the earth, and such as are in the sea, and all that are in them, heard I saying, Blessing, and honour, and glory, and power, be unto him that sitteth upon the throne, and unto the Lamb for ever and ever" (verse 13).

John was told that he would be shown things that would take place in the future. Like we saw in Daniel, we will get the revealed secrets of God from John's day until the end. John 14:1 reminds us of God's promise that He will always be with us and tell us what we need to know to be prepared: "Let not your heart be troubled: ye believe in God, believe also in me." Therefore, we are given encouragement and reassurance that the Lamb's sacrifice is sufficient and will redeem God's chosen people. We have seen the general time outline and the condition of the church during these periods. Now with the opening of the seals, we will obtain some additional details concerning world conditions and what will be the conditions that will confront God's people in a world controlled by Satan's forces. As we saw in the outline of the churches, the admonition is to hold fast and overcome. We are in for a very rough and terrifying time, but God is able to protect us if we trust and obey as did Daniel and the three worthies.

"And I saw when the Lamb opened one of the seals, and I heard ... one of the four beasts saying, Come and see. And I saw, and behold, a white horse: and he that sat on him had a bow; and a crown was given unto him: and he went forth conquering, and to conquer" (Rev. 6:1, 2). We see this same picture in Revelation 19:11, which states, "And I saw heaven opened, and behold a white horse; and he that sat upon him was called Faithful and True, and in righteousness he doth judge and make war."

These seals represent the spiritual warfare that God's people will encounter from the time of Christ's proclamation to "go ye therefore, and teach all nations" (Matt. 28:19) until the angel proclaims "that there should be time no longer" (Rev. 10:6) because "he that is unjust, let him be unjust still ... and he that is righteous, let him be righteous still" (Rev. 22:11).

The white horse of purity and the truth of God during the apostolic age of the church to AD 100 gave way to the red horse of power that took "peace from the earth, and that they should kill one another: and there was given unto him a great sword" (Rev. 6:4). Under this second seal, AD 100–323, the red horse, a symbol of bloodshed, brought about persecution for ten days, which was equal to ten years of tribulation under pagan emperors. Paul wrote these words: "For I know this, that after my departing shall grievous wolves enter in among you, not sparing the flock" (Acts 20:29).

What is this seal's symbolic meaning for me? Have I put aside the purity of God's Word and faith in Him who is the Creator and peace giver and accepted the lying wonders of the father of lies? Am I now persecuting the faithful and true in my state of denial of being deceived? Isn't that what Paul was doing prior to his conversion on the road to Damascus? Sometimes we need physical blindness in order to be able to see spiritually. Stephen's plain words of truth didn't convince Paul of God's reality at that time, which is more than just seeing, tasting, and feeling as we have been studying.

The third seal, the black horse, AD 323–538, represents the great spiritual darkness that progressed as the apostasy deepened, which God predicted in the Old Testament. "But it shall come to pass, if thou wilt not hearken unto the voice of the LORD thy God, to observe to do all his commandments … that all these curses shall come upon thee … And thou shall grope at noonday, as the blind gropeth in darkness" (Deut. 28:15, 29); "For, behold, the darkness shall cover the earth, and gross darkness the people" (Isa. 60:2).

Our secular history refers to this period of earth's history as the Dark Ages. The Word of God, which is the light of the world, was stifled during this period of time and kept from the people. Hosea 4:6 states, "My people are destroyed for lack of knowledge: because thou hast rejected knowledge, I will also reject thee, that thou shalt be no priest to me: seeing thou hast forgotten the law of thy God, I will also forget thy children." He goes on to write, "O Israel, return unto the LORD thy God; for thou hast fallen by thy iniquity.… Who is wise, and he shall understand these things? prudent, and he shall know them? for the ways of the LORD are right, and the just shall walk in them: but the transgressors shall fall therein" (Hosea 14:1, 9).

There are false prophets, teachers, doctrines, as well as false visions and messengers that will extinguish the love of God if we nurture these things. Let us make sure that we believe only the truth as given by the Holy Spirit through the prophets of the living God.

The fourth seal, the pale horse, AD 538–1517, characterizes the time from the beginning to the end of the Reformation during which there is a union of church and state, resulting in great and deadly persecution. This rider is described as "Death, and Hell followed with him. And power was given unto them over the fourth part of the earth, to kill with the sword, and with hunger, and with death, and with the beasts of the earth" (Rev. 6:8).

This period of history corresponds to Daniel's "little horn" reign. A persecution of God's true followers by a power that received its authority from Satan but claimed to be the true church. It killed with the sword of false doctrine while claiming to be "the word." It also destroyed by starving the people of the truth by keeping the Word of God from them. The main time frame of this rider has passed, but it still has an application for us today. There are places all over this earth where truth is suppressed and persecution persists, where false doctrines are believed and forced on the people. Matthew 7:21–23 states, "Not every one that saith unto me Lord, Lord, shall enter into the kingdom of heaven … Many will say to me in that day, Lord, Lord, have we not prophesied in thy name? and in thy name have cast out devils? and in thy name done many wonderful works? And then will I profess unto them, I never knew you: depart from me, ye that work iniquity."

Remember James and John's mistake? "And when his disciples James and John saw this, they said, Lord, wilt thou that we command fire to come down from heaven, and consume them, even as Elias did? But he turned, and rebuked them, and said, Ye know not what manner of spirit ye are of. For the Son of man is not come to destroy men's lives, but to save them" (Luke 9:54–56).

The wicked will be punished in the end, but we humans do not have the ability to judge a persons' fate from our encounter with them. The admonition for us is to "search the scriptures" (John 5:39), "hold fast [to] that which is good" (1 Thess. 5:21), receive Him while we can, and to remember that "if they have persecuted me, they will also persecute you" (John 15:20).

The fifth seal, AD 1517–1755, is a period from the Reformation to the great Lisbon earthquake of November 1, 1755. We are told the following regarding the fifth seal: "I saw under the altar the souls of them that were slain for the word of God, and for the testimony which they held: And they cried with a loud voice, saying, How long, O Lord, holy and true, dost thou not judge and avenge our blood on them that dwell on the earth? And white robes were given unto every one of them; and it was said unto them, that they should rest yet a little season, until their fellowservants also and their brethren, that should be killed as they were, should be fulfilled" (Rev. 6:9–11).

These martyred believers are symbolized as being under the altar and are those slain under the fifth seal. They died for their faith. The figure of personification is used in speaking about Abel in Genesis 4:10, which states "the voice of thy brother's blood crieth unto me from the ground."

Those who have died in the faith are to rest in the grave yet a little while. Daniel's 2300 days didn't end until 1844, and then the judgment began. More persecution was to follow. The resurrection isn't until the last trumpet sounds, which we will be reviewing later.

The sixth seal, AD 1755 to the end, is the opening of the end times and the closing of it.

> And ... there was a great earthquake; and the sun became black as sackcloth of hair, and the moon became as blood; and the stars of heaven fell unto the earth, even as a fig tree casteth her untimely figs, when she is shaken by a mighty wind. And the heavens departed as a scroll when it is rolled together; and every mountain and island were moved out of their places. And the kings of the earth, and the great men, and the rich men, and the chief captains, and the mighty men, and every bondman, and every free man, hid themselves in the dens and in the rocks of the mountains; and said to the mountains and rocks, Fall on us, and hide us from the face of him that sitteth on the throne, and from the wrath of the Lamb: For the great day of his wrath is come; and who shall be able to stand? (Rev. 6:12–17)

The great earthquake of Lisbon that occurred on November 1, 1755, shook an area of four million square miles. In the city of Lisbon nearly 100,000 people were killed. On May 19, 1780, it was so dark at midday that lamps were lit and the chickens went to roost;

that night the moon was blood red.

The Old Testament predicted such signs: "Seek him that … maketh the day dark with night" (Amos 5:8); "For the stars of heaven and the constellations thereof shall not give their light: the sun shall be darkened in his going forth, and the moon shall not cause her light to shine" (Isa. 13:10; see also Isa. 2:19, 21); and "When I shall put thee out, I will cover the heaven, and make the stars thereof dark; I will cover the sun with a cloud, and the moon shall not give her light" (Ezek. 32:7).

The signs of Jesus' coming are also predicted in the New Testament: "Immediately after the tribulation of those days shall the sun be darkened, and the moon shall not give her light, and the stars shall fall from heaven, and the powers of the heavens shall be shaken" (Matt. 24:29) and "The sun shall be turned into darkness, and the moon into blood, before the great and notable day of the Lord come" (Acts 2:20; see also Joel 2:31).

Revelation 7 is a break in the opening of the seals. Under the sixth seal, we have noted that this period extends to the very end of time. We have been seeing what has happened to God's children during the years from Christ to the end.

The Sealing of God's People

Now we are introduced to the sealing of God's people. Notice in Revelation 7:1–3 that the "four angels standing on the four corners of the earth" are told to hold "the four winds" until "we have sealed the servants of our God in their foreheads." (See Daniel 7:2, where it talks about the winds of strife.) John had been giving details of the persecution of God's people. He has just told of celestial events that would signal the nearness of the end of time and how the wicked of all classes, ranks, and status would react to Christ's coming wrath. We find that God has provided a method of security for His people. They are to be sealed in their foreheads. Just as the Israelites were protected from the plagues God sent upon the Egyptians at the time of the exodus, the people of God will be protected from the seven last plagues that will be poured out upon the wicked prior to Christ's coming. By faith, the Israelites marked the doorposts with the blood of the sacrificial lamb, and by faith and our actions, we show that we are worthy to be sealed by Christ's blood. Revelation 7:4 states, "And I heard the number of them which were sealed: and there were sealed an hundred and forty and four thousand of all the tribes of the children of Israel," twelve thousand from each tribe.

As stated previously, the numbers seven and twelve denote completeness, and thousands denote a vast number. Historically, as seen in the various censuses, the numbers given for the various tribes were never the same number of individuals per tribe. Also, when Christ comes there will be believers who aren't of the strict blood lineage of the twelve tribes. Therefore, I believe these tribes are symbolic. Galatians 3:28 teaches us that "there is neither Jew nor Greek, there is neither bond nor free, there is neither male nor female: for ye are all one in Christ Jesus." And we read in Revelation 14:12 that those who inherit the kingdom are people who "keep the commandments of God, and the faith of Jesus." God is not a respecter of persons as we have previously seen. Therefore, those who love God and love their fellow human beings and keep the faith of Jesus will be counted worthy to be sealed. Thus, they will not receive the plagues of wrath that will be poured out upon the wicked.

Then the scene changes from the protective sealing work of God's last generation of believers on earth to heaven's throne room.

After this I looked, and there before me was a great multitude that no one could count, from every nation, tribe, people and language, standing before the throne and before the Lamb. They were wearing white robes and were holding palm branches in their hands. And they cried out in a loud voice: "Salvation belongs to our God, who sits on the throne, and to the Lamb." All the angels were standing around the throne and around the elders and the four living creatures. They fell down on their faces before the throne and worshiped God, saying: "Amen! Praise and glory and wisdom and thanks and honor and power and strength be to our God for ever and ever Amen!"

Then one of the elders asked me, "These in the white robes—who are they, and where did they come from?" I answered, "Sir, you know." And he said, "These are they who have come out of the great tribulation; they have washed their robes and made them white in the blood of the Lamb. Therefore, "they are before the throne of God and serve him day and night in his temple; ... 'Never again will they hunger; ... thirst. The sun will not beat down on them, ' nor any scorching heat. For the Lamb at the center of the throne will be their shepherd; ... 'And God will wipe away every tear from their eyes.'" (Rev. 7:9–17, NIV)

We are under this seal today. Are we submitting ourselves to be sealed, or are we looking for hiding places? On the other hand, in our complacency, are we refusing to believe we are in any danger? Remember, this is also the era of the Laodicean church who says, I am rich and do not need anything! "Wherefore let him that thinketh he standeth take heed lest he fall" (1 Cor. 10:12).

Our self-sacrificing God loves us so much that He gave His Son Jesus to die in our place that we might have everlasting life as His created and adopted sons and daughters. John wrote, "And let him that is athirst come. And whosoever will, let him take of the water of life freely" (Rev. 22:17). What is your choice?

Revelation 8:1 describes the last or seventh seal, which is the coming of Christ and the close of this earth's history: "And when he had opened the seventh seal, there was silence in heaven about the space of half an hour." In Matthew 25:31 we read about His glorious appearing: "When the Son of man shall come in his glory, and all the holy angels with him, then shall he sit upon the throne of his glory." It is easy to understand why there is silence in heaven for about half an hour. There is no one there. All the beings of heaven have come with Christ for that glorious welcoming of all the redeemed. Oh, what a glorious moment! That which was lost will finally be restored.

When Jesus returns in the clouds of glory, God's character will finally be vindicated. We can understand the scene in heaven under the sixth seal of the "great multitude, which no man could number, of all nations, and kindreds, and people, and tongues" (Rev. 7:9). These are God's people from Adam to the last person who surrenders to God's will. The reign of disobedience, with all its ramifications, is over and God's love and peace will reign once again over all creation.

It's sad that our study does not end here on this happy note. We are told that John has a lot more details for us of those "things which must shortly come to pass" (Rev. 1:1). We can take heart and encouragement from the glimpses we have seen to carry us through the conflicts that befall believers until the end of time. God is still in control of events on earth, and we can overcome through obedience to Him that created all things. Let's continue with the details given John concerning world conditions and their effects on the righteous and those who are in rebellion against God's principles.

The Seven Trumpets

The seven trumpets are described in Revelation chapters 8 through 10. Trumpets are symbols of war and trouble (Jer. 4:19; 1 Cor. 14:8). Like Daniel these trumpets are symbolic of the rise and fall of empires, kingdoms, and religious powers. Please read *The History of the Decline and Fall of the Roman Empire* by Edward Gibbon and *The Prophecies of Daniel and the Revelation* by Uriah Smith, for both books go into great historical detail, which enforces the accuracy of these facts. It is from Smith's book that most of the historical facts are gleaned for this study.

The first four trumpets deal with the downfall of the Roman Empire that ruled the world from before Christ, the fifth and sixth with the downfall of the Eastern Division of Rome, and the seventh with the downfall of all the kingdoms of this world. Go back and review Daniel's interpretation of Nebuchadnezzar's dream of the image of a man. The legs of iron represent the two divisions of the Roman Empire, which are later the ten kingdoms before the Rock crushes them.

- First Trumpet (AD 395–410) – Alaric and then Goths invaded the Roman Empire from the North.

- Second Trumpet (AD) 428–476) – Genseric with the Vandals invade African provinces and Italy from the sea, destroying the Roman fleet of more than 1,000 ships and more than 100,000 men.

- Third Trumpet (AD 451) – The western empire was invaded by the Huns under Attila. He called himself the "Scourge of God." "It was the boast of Attila that the grass never grew on the spot which his horse had trod…. And the concluding paragraph of the chapters which record his history, is entitled, 'Symptoms of Decay and Ruin of the Roman Government.' The name of the star is called Wormwood" (Smith, *The Prophecies of Daniel and the Revelation*, p. 487).

- Fourth Trumpet (AD 476) – Western Rome fell at the hands of the Heruli under Odoacer. Italy then became a province of the Emperor of Eastern Rome, ruling from Constantinople.

- Fifth Trumpet – These are the "woes," and they refer to their devastating character. Mohammed and conquests of Islam against Eastern Rome took place in this period. On July 7, 1299, Othman invaded the territory of Eastern Rome, a territory in which there was no central government until he assumed control. This power had power to "hurt men for five months or 150 years." July 27, 1299 plus 150 years brings us to July 27, 1449. The eastern section of the Roman Empire was not politically killed, but it was tormented.

- Sixth Trumpet – The four angels or

messengers are explained as four Sultanates—Bagdad, Iconium, Aleppo, and Damascus—situated in the valley of the Euphrates (see Rev. 16:12–16; 7:1–3). The Turks, now the leading power, took Constantinople and overcame the last remnant of Roman power in AD 1453. Gunpowder was used in this battle.

Another time prophecy is given in Revelation 9:15: "And the four angels were loosed, which were prepared for an hour, and a day, and a month, and a year, for to slay the third part of men." A hour equals fifteen days; a day equals one year; a month equals thirty years; and a year equals 360 years, for a total of 391 years and 15 days. When added to July 27, 1449, we arrive at August 11, 1840.

In 1449 the emperor of Constantinople died, and before his brother, Constantine XIII, took the throne, he asked permission of Amurth, the Turkish Sultan. Thus, the independence of the Eastern Empire was voluntarily surrendered to the Turks. On August 11, 1840, (391 years and 15 days later), the Turks, for all intents and purposes, surrendered their independence into the hands of the European powers. Mehmet Ali Pasha of Egypt, ruler under the authority of the Sultan, was about to overthrow the Sultan himself; whereupon the Sultan put his affairs in the hands of England, Russia, Austria, and Prussia. On August 11, 1840, the Ottoman Empire collapsed and the prophecy was fulfilled.

Here is where we stand today in the kingdoms of the toes. Daniel had prophesied that miry clay and iron do not mix (Dan. 2:43). There has been royal weddings and wars, but those seven words hold true. There will not be another world kingdom before Jesus comes.

This brings us to the seventh trumpet. "But in the days of the voice of the seventh angel, when he shall begin to sound, the mystery of God should be finished, as he hath declared to his servants the prophets" (Rev. 10:7). "I certify you, brethren, that the gospel which was preached of me is not after man. For I neither received it of man, neither was I taught it, but by the revelation of Jesus Christ" (Gal. 1:11, 12). The mystery of God is mentioned in Ephesians 3:3–6: "That is, the mystery made known to me by revelation, as I have already written briefly. In reading this, then, you will be able to understand my insight into the mystery of Christ, which was not made known to people in other generations as it has now been revealed by the Spirit to God's holy apostles and prophets. This mystery is that through the gospel the Gentiles are heirs together with Israel, members together of one body, and sharers together in the promise in Christ Jesus" (NIV).

The mystery of God is the good news of the gospel, which is salvation and redemption with restoration of all things through "the Lamb slain from the foundation of the world" (Rev. 13:8)—Jesus Christ. "And the seventh angel sounded; and there were great voices in heaven, saying, The kingdoms of this world are become the kingdoms of our Lord, and of his Christ; and he shall reign for ever and ever" (Rev. 11:15). This is the fulfillment of the great rock in Daniel's vision that is cut out without hands. His kingdom will crush everyone who does not follow the Lamb and last forever.

This is a brief overview of world conditions from the time of Christ until the end of time. Most of this information has been social and political in nature, and now we shall examine the spiritual warfare that Satan will wage by and through world governments to persecute God's people. Please read what Jesus reveals

A Study of God's Love & Mankind's History

to His disciples in Matthew 24, Mark 13, and Luke 21. These are the general signs and conditions that will affect His people at the end of earth's history. John is given more details to share with believers, and these, in combination with what the Holy Spirit revealed to Daniel, help us to understand these messages.

Chapter 8
False Worship/Assembling

Satan's False Church

In Revelation 12 Satan, acting through pagan Rome, is portrayed as a dragon, and the pure, true church is represented as a pregnant woman who is "clothed with the sun" (the New Testament, gospel era) with the "moon under her feet" (the Old Testament Mosaic period), while wearing a "crown of twelve stars" (the apostles) on her head (verse 1).

Just as Satan, the serpent, devoured Eve with his subtleness, he now is pictured ready to devour the child the woman is about to deliver. Satan, acting through Herod, tried to kill Jesus as a baby when he ordered the execution of all male babies two years and under in Bethlehem (Matt. 2:16).

"And the woman fled into the wilderness, where she hath a place prepared of God, that they should feed her there a thousand two hundred and threescore days.... And to the woman were given two wings of the great eagle, that she might fly into the wilderness, into her place, where she is nourished for a time, and times, and a half time, from the face of the serpent" (Rev. 12:6, 14).

Notice that these periods of time are the same as seen in Daniel's prophecies (Dan. 7:25; 12:7). In Revelation 11:2 and 13:5 we find this same period of 1260 years referred to as "forty and two months." The beginning of this time was noted in Daniel when the papacy was firmly established in AD 538. And yet, in the midst of persecution, God's people, the true believers, were whisked to safety "on eagles wings." "Ye have seen what I did unto the Egyptians, and how I bare you on eagles' wings, and brought you unto myself" (Exod. 19:4).

Hear what Paul says in 2 Thessalonians: "Let no man deceive you by any means: for *that day shall not come*, except there come a falling away first, and that man of sin be revealed, the son of perdition; Who opposeth and exalteth himself above all that is called God, or that is worshipped; so that he as God sitteth in the temple of God, shewing himself that he is God.... For the mystery of iniquity doth already work: only he who now letteth *will let*, until he be taken out of the way" (2 Thess. 2:3–7, emphasis added).

That ecclesiastic church who during all the Dark Ages trumpeted her lordly commands into the ears of listening Christendom was not the church of Christ; it was the body of the mystery of iniquity. This continues to be true.

"And the serpent cast out of his mouth water as a flood after the woman, that he might cause her to be carried away of the flood" (Rev. 12:15). Isaiah predicted that "when the enemy shall come in like a flood, the Spirit of the LORD shall lift up a standard against him."

It isn't a secret that false doctrines, teachers, preachers have been around since the fall. Therefore, Paul wrote, "That we henceforth be no more children, tossed to and fro, and carried about with every wind of doctrine, by the sleight of men, and cunning craftiness, whereby they lie in wait to deceive" (Eph. 4:14). "But there were false prophets also among the people, even as there shall be false teachers among you, who privily shall bring in damnable heresies, even denying the Lord that bought them, and bring upon themselves swift destruction. And many shall follow their pernicious ways; by reason of whom the way of truth shall be evil spoken of" (2 Peter 2:1, 2). Christ also warned about deception, saying, "For false Christs and false prophets shall arise, and shall shew signs and wonders, to seduce, if it were possible, even the elect" (Mark 13:22). "For the time will come when they will not endure sound doctrine; but after their own lusts shall they heap to themselves teachers, having itching ears; and they shall turn away their ears from the truth, and shall be turned unto fables" (2 Tim. 4:3, 4).

The great flood of false doctrines that issued from the papacy and corrupted all nations produced, as it were, absolute control of the civil powers for many centuries. The Protestant Reformation of the sixteenth century began to enlighten the masses. Martin Luther and others exposed some of the true nature of the papacy. Men began to exercise and regulate their consciences by God's Word alone. Defenders of the true faith multiplied. Soon there was enough Protestant soil found in Europe and the New World to swallow up the flood of papal fury and rob it of its power to harm the church.

However, the dragon was not through with his work and Revelation 12:17 states that the dragon "went to make war with the remnant of her seed, which keep the commandments of God, and have the testimony of Jesus Christ." Even though for 1260 years the papacy exercised its power over the lives of people by force of excommunication, torture, and death, there still were faithful God-fearing individuals who did not accept the false doctrines and continued to spread the truth as they knew it.

This power in its pagan form (civil government) is now seen as a leopardlike beast coming out of the sea in Revelation 13. Remember, the sea represents peoples or inhabited areas. This beast has all the elements of the world powers before it and also his "mouth speaking great things and blasphemies; and power was given unto him to continue forty and two months" (verse 5). Here the civil persecution gives away to religious persecution. "The dragon gave him his power, and his seat, and great authority.... And they worshipped the dragon which gave power unto the beast: and they worshipped the beast ... And it was given unto him to make war with the saints, and to overcome them: and power was given him over all kindreds, and tongues, and nations. And all that dwell upon the earth shall worship him, whose names are not written in the book of life of the Lamb slain from the foundation of the world" (verses 2–8).

Paul warned Timothy about the character traits of men in the last days: "This know also, that in the last days perilous times shall come. For men shall be lovers of their own selves, covetous, boasters, proud, blasphemers, disobedient to parents, unthankful, unholy, without natural affection, trucebreakers, false accusers, incontinent, fierce, despisers of those that are good, traitors, heady, highminded, lovers of pleasures more than lovers of God; having a form of godliness, but denying the power thereof: from such turn away.... Ever learning, and never able to come to the knowledge of truth" (2 Tim. 3:1–7). "For the time will come when they will not endure sound doctrine; but after their own lusts shall they heap to themselves teachers, having itching ears; and they shall turn away their ears from the truth, and shall be turned unto fables" (2 Tim. 4:3, 4).

Both the dragon and the leopardlike beast represent the Roman Empire. The dragon represents the civil authority, and the beast represents the ecclesiastic authority of Rome. We see the beginning of this dual relationship at the time of Constantine's conversion to Christianity and his influence on matters of religion. Persecution largely ceased, and he made the first Sunday law when he issued the following on March 7, AD 321: "Let all judges and town people, and the occupation of all trades rest on the venerable day of the sun; but let those who are situated in the country, freely and at full liberty, attend to the business of agriculture; because it often happens that no other day is so fit for sowing corn and planting vines; lest the critical moment being let slip, men should lose the commodities granted by heaven" (Corpus Juris Civilis Cod.: lib. 3, tit. 12,3).

Thus, a fusing of church and state took place. The "church" gained the controlling power with the breakup of the Roman Empire. However, this church's power was not controlled by God; "the dragon gave him his power, and his seat, and great authority" (Rev. 13:2). This beast power (false church) was given power "to make war [persecute] with the saints, and to overcome them." Just as Israel failed to follow God and His doctrines, the church allowed the false doctrines of Satan to enter into and mingle with the truth of God, which resulted in the mixed wine of her fornication. Kings ruled with the blessings from this ecclesiastic power of Rome, and it was the dragon that gave this "church" its power.

The United States in Prophecy and the Mark of the Beast

The scene now shifts and we, with John, see another beast, only this time it is "coming up out of the earth":

And he had two horns like a lamb, and he spake as a dragon. And he exerciseth all the power of the first beast before him, and causeth the earth and them which dwell therein to worship the first beast, whose deadly wound was healed. And he doeth great wonders, so that he maketh fire come down from heaven on the earth in the sight of men, And deceiveth them that dwell on the earth by the means of those miracles which he had power to do in the sight of the beast; saying to them that dwell on the earth, that they should make an image to the beast, which had the wound by a sword, and did live. And he had power to give life unto the image of the beast, that the image of the beast should both speak, and cause that as many as would not worship the image of the beast should be killed. And he causeth all, both small and great, rich and poor, free and bond, to receive a mark in their right hand, or in their foreheads: And that no man might buy or sell, save he that had the mark, or the name of the beast, or the number of his name. Here is wisdom. Let him that hath understanding count the number of the beast: for it is the number of a man; and his number is Six hundred threescore and six. (Rev. 13:11–18)

This beast did not uproot another nation, but it gradually expanded in a somewhat peaceful manner. God's principles were woven into the Constitution, and instead of a horn representing a kingdom, this beast power had two horns, which represents the two branches of government that make the laws and by which it speaks. This is a representative form of government, a republic, that is governed by the people. This beast, of course, is representing the United States of America, which has been lamblike up until this point, but it will soon "speak as a dragon." This power will exercise the power of the first beast and cause all to worship the first beast.

The first beast represents the papacy, which received a deadly wound in 1798 when the papal government was for a time abolished by the taking of Pope Pius VI prisoner by General Berthier. The pope died in exile. On March 14, 1800, a new pope was elected and the papacy was reestablished, but with less of its former power.

Remember, again, the statement that "all the world wondered after the beast" (Rev. 13:3). How much influence does the papacy have on the nations of the world? Much more than a casual look into the Holy See would produce. The United States has had a personal presidential envoy to the Vatican since President Franklin Roosevelt. This was upgraded to an ambassadorship in 1983. The Catholic Church has adherents in all nations, and its goal is to make converts by influencing national leaders to be favorable toward it. They have the secular power behind them to enforce their doctrine. At the same time, national leaders try to influence the Vatican to endorse their international programs. In an article by Thomas J. Reese titled "Three Years Later: U.S. Relations with the Holy See" and published in *America* on January 17, 1987, it was written that "the Vatican wishes to do whatever it can to safeguard the ability of Catholics to practice, to worship according to their beliefs."

The Catholic Church promotes the commandments of men gilded in the wrappings of truth. Notice that this is to safeguard "their beliefs," not the right for each to chose their own beliefs or the worship of the true creator God. This is that power to which an image is to be made and all are commanded to worship on pain of death. Yes, God is jealous of His laws, doctrines, and truths. "Thou shalt have no other gods before me" (Exod. 20:3). He is intolerant in this and rigid in His ways, for they are righteous. The choice is yours. Who will you follow?

The First Amendment to the Constitution begins, "Congress shall make no law respecting an establishment of religion, or prohibiting the free exercise thereof." This is, also, representative of the two horn's "civil" and "religious" powers that we have in the United States of America. There is supposed to be a separation of church and state, but we find that there is an infringement on the rights of the church by the state rather than by the church on the state at this point. There are no definite laws in force at this time to "establish" one church or denomination as the "state church." However, there are those who seek to deny others the right to these freedoms to promote the gospel message and the principles of sound doctrine. To say "thus saith the Lord" is considered intolerant, bigoted, hateful, and hypocritical, etc., and worst of all, not loving the God we love, profess, and uphold. The accuser of the brethren is still hard at work.

The "lie" is ever present in the form of excuses that anything goes: "I'm only human"; "What two consenting adults do is all right"; 'Just do it"; "I'm OK, you are OK"; "It's my right"; "If it feels good, do it"; "I'm worth it"; "Just once won't hurt"; "Try it, you'll like it"; and you know of others as well. I read sometime ago a statement that reflects this attitude; it went something like this, "As long as sin is engaged in, a person will search the Scriptures for a justification to continue in sinning." The Scriptures are badly twisted by many to fit their brand of "belief."

The wise counsel is "be not deceived." The Jews of Jesus' time, just one week before His death, had shouted "Hosanna" (Matt. 21:9). A week later they were shouting, "Let him be crucified" (Matt. 27:23). They had the scriptures and the prophets, but they didn't know the Lord that had given them. Yet, "the centurion, and they that were with him ... [said], Truly this was the Son of God" (verse 54).

Will you be on the wrong side of the issue when the decree is proclaimed that those who do "not worship the image of the beast should be killed" (Rev. 13:15)? This is the same type of law the three worthies faced that led to their being thrown in the fiery furnace, and Daniel faced that led him to be thrown into the lion's den.

Those who are deceived receive a mark on the forehead or in the hand. What is this mark? We have seen that the papacy, the beast, the little horn, and the first beast are all names for the same "power." John, writing what was revealed to him hundreds of years before it would happen, declared that the number of the beast power would be 666. This beast power, as we have seen, has certain characteristics. It speaks "great things and blasphemies ... against God, ... his name, and his tabernacle, and them that dwell in heaven" (Rev. 13:5, 6). Jesus was accused of blasphemy when He said He was the Son of God, which He was and is, and when He forgave sins, which was in His authority to do so (see John 10:33; Luke 5:21). We have seen that this beast power received "his power, and his seat, and great authority" (Rev. 13:2), not from God, but from "the dragon," Satan.

This power then is ecclesiastical in nature, not civil or secular. What ecclesiastic power could have been in power for 1260 years, at which time it wore out the saints, made war against them, and changed times and laws, then received a deadly wound but is still alive? This all fits the papacy. Does the name 666 fit the papacy? It is well documented that the official Latin title for the pope is Vicarius Filii Dei. It means Vicar of the Son of God. The use of Roman numerals for the letters in that title adds up as follows: v/u=10; i=6; c=100; l=50; d=500; for a total of 666. Can a mortal man sit in the place of God? Can this man forgive sins? Isn't that what Lucifer tried to do in heaven? The pope has no authority or power to forgive sins, nor should he accept the worship of others, yet many people bow to his authority.

We must fall before the cross of Calvary with a broken and contrite heart, confessing our sins to the crucified Savior and ask forgiveness of Him. By repenting of our sins with genuine remorse, we can accept the new heart that He will give us and be able to come boldly before the throne of grace to accept the Father's tender mercy that He so lovingly wishes to bestow upon us. Christ, our advocate and redeemer, will be by our side pleading for and with us. The pope cannot do that for us, and no amount of deeds of penitence or hail Mary's will suffice.

At this time the two-horned beast (the United States) has not declared that an image to the first beast (the papacy) should be made or worshipped. The lamblike beast is currently in control. However, how long will it be before the dragon begins to exercise his voice? The tolerance of evil practices in the name of freedom of expression has eroded morality to the point where Satan's voice is the accepted standard, and he is about to roar and devour God's followers. What would constitute this image?

Going back to Nebuchadnezzar's image that was set up, it was all of gold. He had forgotten who rules in the affairs of men and kings (and popes). Daniel 4:30 states, "Is not this great Babylon, that I have built for the house of the kingdom by the might of my power, and for the honour of my majesty?" His pride was also Satan's pride.

In Matthew 23:11 Jesus said, "But he that is greatest among you shall be your servant." He also said, "Verily, verily, I say unto you, The servant is not greater than his lord; neither he that is sent greater than he that sent him" (John 13:16). The papacy has exalted a man to a status above the Lord whom it claims to serve. It was prophesied in Daniel that the beast would try to change times and laws, which referred to God's laws, not civil laws. But what was changed? We know that it has to do with worship. Do we have any evidence of such changes? Do you remember Constantine's decree in AD 321? Let's look further into what the Catholic Church says about these changes.

The Decalogue as recorded in Exodus 20:3–17 contains four commandments that have to do with worship and love for and to God. In *The Convert's Catechism of Catholic Doctrine*, we find that the second commandment is missing. This is the commandment that tells us that we should not make and worship images. Also, the tenth commandment is split in half in order to made up for the removal of the second commandment. Lastly, the fourth commandment, which is listed as third, is shortened to simply read, "Remember that thou keep holy the Sabbath day."

By removing the second commandment and shortening the fourth commandment, men have changed God's law and made it so that He is not identifiable. Also, with no law against image worship, then an image to the beast would be permissible and proper. As John wrote in 1 John 3:4: "Whosoever committeth sin transgresseth also the law: for sin is the transgression of the law."

Let's put God back into the picture and into the Ten Commandments. The fourth commandment reads, "Remember the sabbath day, to keep it holy. Six days shalt thou labour, and do all thy work: But the seventh day is the sabbath of the Lord thy God: in it thou shalt not do any work, thou, nor thy son, nor thy daughter, thy manservant, nor thy maidservant, nor thy cattle, nor thy stranger that is within thy gates: For in six days the Lord made heaven and earth. the sea, and all that in them is, and rested the seventh day:

wherefore the Lord blessed the sabbath day, and hallowed it" (Exod. 20:8–11).

God lays it out plainly and simply. No need to guess or try to interpret what has been said. This is the same seventh day that God blessed and sanctified when He finished His creation work (Gen. 2:1–3). This seventh day is the day on which no manna fell from heaven for forty years (Exod. 16:4–6, 22–26). God did this to prove or test them to see if they would obey His laws. It also showed them that God can provide and sustain under any condition. Please note that this was before the Lord God wrote the Ten Commandments on the tablets of stone.

Also, we find that the principles of the Ten Commandments were known and recorded before they were given in written form on Mount Sinai. Consider this list:

1. First commandment – "Make there an altar unto God" (Gen. 35:2)

2. Second commandment – "Put away the strange gods" (Gen. 35:2)

3. Third commandment – "Neither shalt thou profane the name of thy God" (Lev. 18:21)

4. Fourth commandment – The Sabbath day was blessed and sanctified (Gen. 2:1–4; Exod. 16:22–30)

5. Fifth commandment – An example of dishonoring one's parent and the curse that follows (Gen. 9:22–25)

6. Sixth commandment – You should not hurt or kill anyone (Gen. 4:8–11, 23, 24; 9:5, 6)

7. Seventh commandment – You should remain faithful to your spouse (Gen. 20:5–9; 38:24; 39:7–9)

8. Eighth commandment – You should not take what doesn't belong to you (Gen. 30:33; 31:19, 30, 32, 39; 44:8)

9. Ninth commandment – You should not lie (Gen. 3:4; 39:7–20)

10. Tenth commandment – You need to be content with what you have. If someone has broken the eighth commandment, they have broken this one as well.

Just as we find these principles before the formal writing on the tablets of stone by God's own finger, we are able to find them in the New Testament after Christ's resurrection. Why is this important? Because the papacy "thinks" to change laws, and God's Word proves that it is the same from beginning to end. Examine these verses in the New Testament for proof of God's unchanging law: (1) Acts 14:11–15; 1 Corinthians 8:4–6; (2) 1 Corinthians 10:14; Acts 17:29; 1 John 5:21; (3) James 5:12; (4) Hebrews 4:9; Acts 16:13; Acts 17:2; (5) Ephesians 6:2; (6–10) Romans 13:9. We continue to see that God and His principles do not change. That is part of His characteristics. Any changes would have to be from a false authority!

As we have seen, God's people are to be sealed "in their foreheads" (Rev. 7:1–3; 14:1; Ezek. 9:1–6). And the followers of the beast will receive a mark "in his forehead, or in his hand" (Rev. 14:9). Those seals or marks distinguish who or what we worship and whom we belong to. A seal shows three things: (1) The name of the person or law giver; (2) his official position, title, or right to rule; and (3) his kingdom or territory over which he rules. The fourth commandment is the only commandment that meets these three requirements and reveals the seal of God. The fourth commandment reveals the name of the person we worship, God. His title is that of Creator of the universe. And the extent of His domain is heaven and earth.

Furthermore, in Exodus 31:13–17, God says, "Speak thou also unto the children of Israel, saying, Verily my sabbaths ye shall keep: for it is a sign between me and you throughout your generations; that ye may know that I am the LORD that doth sanctify you.... Wherefore the children of Israel shall keep the sabbath, to observe the sabbath throughout their generations, for a perpetual covenant. It is a sign between me and the children of Israel for ever."

Do not be deceived into thinking that the seventh-day Sabbath was only for the Jews and that Christians today are to worship on Sunday, the first day of the week. Galatians 3:29 states, "And if ye be Christ's, then are ye Abraham's seed, and heirs according to the promise." As we just saw in Exodus 16:4, the reason no manna fell on the Sabbath was to prove their sincerity in being obedient to God by walking in His law.

God set the Sabbath apart from the rest of the weekdays to worship Him and communicate with Him. It is a sign or seal that we are obedient to His commandments and we acknowledge that He is to be worshipped. It isn't any day that we choose. It is a specific day, the seventh day, and it was called the Sabbath. It was only the seventh day that was blessed, sanctified, and hallowed, not any of the other days. On this point, remember that our God is the same yesterday, today, and forever.

In Isaiah 66:22, 23, God said, "For as the new heavens and the new earth, which I will make, shall remain before me, saith the LORD, so shall your seed and your name remain. And it shall come to pass, that from one new moon to another, and from one sabbath to another, shall all flesh come to worship before me." The Sabbath, the seventh day of the week, Saturday, is God's seal or mark of authority.

Does the papacy have some day it claims that would satisfy the requirement of thinking to change laws? The answer as we have seen is yes. The initial law was given by Constantine in AD 321 to worship on Sunday. We read Canon 29, which was composed around AD 364 by the Council of Laodicea, as is documented in *History of the Sabbath and the First Day of the Week* by John Nevins Andrews: "Christians shall not Judaize and be idle on Saturday [Sabbath, original], but shall work on that day; but the Lord's day they shall especially honor, and, as being Christians, shall, if possible, do no work on that day. If, however, they are found Judaizing, they shall be shut out from Christ."

From Rev. Dr. James Butler's *Catechism* we read, "Question: What day was the Sabbath? Answer: Saturday. Question: Who changed it? Answer: The Catholic Church" (p. 57). And from *A Doctrinal Catechism* by Rev. Stephen Keenan we read, "Question: Have you any other way of proving that the church has power to institute festivals of precept? Answer: Had she not such power she could not have done that in which all modern religionists agree with her; she could not have substituted the observance of Sunday, the first day of the week, for the observance of Saturday, the seventh day; a change for which there is no scriptural authority" (p. 174). And lastly, a quotation from *Plain Talk About the Protestantism of Today* by Mgr. Louis Segur, "It was the Catholic Church which, by the authority of Jesus Christ, has transferred this rest to the Sunday in remembrance of the resurrection of our Lord. Thus the observance of Sunday by the Protestants is a homage they pay, in spite of themselves, to the authority of the [Catholic] Church" (p. 213).

It is clear from Scripture and the Catholic Church that the Sabbath instituted by God is the seventh day of the week, Saturday, as established from the beginning. It does not matter what exalted position a person holds on this earth or how plausible or desirable a "change" appears to be. If it cannot be supported by a clear "thus saith the Lord," it is not from God.

This study is not about individuals or denominations. It is about false doctrines that enslave individuals to a false set of values that go against the Word of God. There is no righteous person; all have sinned. Christ died that all could be redeemed. He says, "Follow Me." He invites everyone to obey Him and His teachings and not be partakers of the wrath He will send upon those who remain stubbornly defiant of His laws when the world comes to an end and He establishes His kingdom. In 1 John 3:4 we are reminded that sin is the transgression of the law, and Jesus reminds us that He came to uphold the law: "Think not that I am come to destroy the law, or the prophets: I am not come to destroy, but to fulfil" (Matt. 5:17). He came to show that love, which the Ten Commandments portray, brings peace and harmony and can be kept, adhered to, obeyed, and lived by. We find that the papacy thought to make the Sabbath change and that most Protestant churches accept this change, thereby, paying homage to the Roman Catholic doctrines.

The judicial laws of the United States of America were largely base on Judeo-Christian principles with an emphasis on tolerance of the other person's beliefs. From its founding, the majority of the population has regarded this as a "Christian" nation and, therefore, has considered Sunday as sacred. There are Sunday laws on the nation's books already. These were labeled "blue laws." They are not being enforced at this time; however, we know that they will be resurrected and enforced when the United States makes the image to the beast that "should both speak, and cause that as many as would not worship the image of the beast should be killed. And he causeth all ... to receive a mark in their right hand, or in their foreheads" (Rev. 13:15, 16).

The groundwork for a national Sunday law has been in the making for years. The decline in the moral standards of the world, in general, along with the movement for more "tolerance" for evil practices sets the stage for the opening scene. The curtain is about to open! As conditions of the world decline, there will be a great effort to correct the trend, but not with God's principles. There will be so-called God or Christian inspired programs that are blindly followed and enforced to address this decadent action, but in reality they will be Satan's programs and will be used to appease those who think they are doing God's will and who have been resisting and speaking out against them. Only those, the elect, the ones who have chosen to follow what the Scriptures say and are fully grounded in the Word, will be able to stand and not be deceived.

We are living in the Laodicean age. Have you opened your eyes spiritually to see that you are "wretched," "miserable," "poor," "blind," and "naked"? Can you see that the Sabbath is a test of loyalty to God? It's your choice, will you obey God or Satan? There is no neutral ground!

The Three Angels Messages—God's Final Pleadings

In Revelation 14:1–5, we see that John has been informed of the final triumph of the faithful. There is righteousness and a reward at the end of this ordeal, but before the end, our attention and John's is turned to three angels flying in the midst of heaven. Each has a message. These angels symbolize the spreading of the everlasting gospel to the whole world. God's people are spreading the messages while their enemies are devising plans for their destruction.

Let's read Revelation 14:6–13:

> And I saw another angel flying in the midst of heaven, having the everlasting gospel to preach unto them that dwell on the earth, and to every nation, and kindred, and tongue, and people, saying with a loud voice, Fear God, and give glory to him; for the hour of his judgment is come: and worship him that made heaven, and earth, and the sea, and the fountains of waters. And there followed another angel, saying, Babylon is fallen, is fallen, that great city, because she made all nations drink of the wine of the wrath of her fornication. And a third angel followed them, saying with a loud voice, If any man worship the beast and his image, and receive his mark in his forehead, or in his hand, the same shall drink: of the wine of the wrath of God, which is poured out without mixture into the cup of his indignation; and he shall be tormented with fire and brimstone in the presence of the holy angels, and in the presence of the Lamb: and the smoke of their torment ascendeth up for ever and ever: and they have no rest day nor night, who worship the beast and his image, and whosoever receiveth the mark of his name. Here is the patience of the saints: here are they that keep the commandments of God, and the faith of Jesus. And I heard a voice from heaven saying unto me, Write, Blessed are the dead which die in the Lord from henceforth: Yea, saith the Spirit, that they may rest from their labours; and their words do follow them.

These messages are continuing and overlapping. They are as valid today as when they were first proclaimed. Notice that it is "the everlasting gospel to preach unto them that dwell on the earth." Jesus gave His disciples the following commission in Matthew 28:19, 20, which matches the call here in Revelation: "Go ye therefore, and teach all nations … to observe all things whatsoever I have commanded you."

This is in opposition to the wine of fornication that the beast and the image offer and that will reap the wrath of God. We are to "fear God," i.e. reverence Him and glorify His name for "the hour of His judgment is come" (Rev. 14:7). We found that Daniel's 2300-day prophecy ended in 1844 when Christ entered into the sanctuary and began His priestly responsibility of judging the people and cleansing the temple.

What other things were occurring during this period of time in the mid-1800s that impacted the first angel's message? There was a worldwide interest from various denominational leaders and others in the nearness of Christ's coming. Serious Bible scholars led in-depth study regarding the second coming of Christ and discovered several important truths that, when added to the other truths already believed, led to the formation of the Seventh-day Adventist Church. It is this church that has been foremost in the spreading of the three angels' messages to the world.

Darwin and his theory of evolution also started in this timeframe; as well as

Joseph Smith's vision and the founding of the Mormon Church.

The second angel's message is about Babylon and how it is fallen, but we shouldn't ascribe this Babylon to just the papacy. While there was a "fall" when Pope Pius VI was captured, placed in exile and then died, Babylon extends to all her daughters, and this power extends to the end of the world. It is in these chapters of Revelation, including chapter 16, that more detail is given as to what will happen to the wicked. Those who are not willing to obey God and come out of Babylon will be recipients of God's wrath. Have you made your decision in regards to God's invitation?

The third angel's messages are about the patience of the saints in keeping the commandments of God and the faith of Jesus; thereby, they have a strong defense against the beast and his image. Can we say with Job 13:15, "Though he slay me, yet will I trust in him"? Even if you don't feel as if you can say this, remember that you can ask God for help as did the father of the child that had the "dumb spirit." He said, "Lord, I believe; help thou mine unbelief" (Mark 9:24).

The Seven Last Plagues; the State of the Dead; and Babylon's Fall

The rest of Revelation 14 deals with the second coming of Christ and the reaping of the world's harvest. In the parable of the harvest, Jesus taught that the "wheat" and the "tares" would grow together until the end when the reapers would gather the "wheat," God's people, into the barn, and take the "tares," the wicked, are burn it (Matt. 13:24–30, 37–43).

Then, in Revelation 15, we read about the seven last plagues. "And I saw another sign in heaven, great and marvellous, seven angels having the seven last plagues; for in them is filled up the wrath of God" (verse 1). Some people question how God can destroy anyone, but Romans 2:5–11 has this to say about the wicked,

> But after thy hardness and impenitent heart treasurest up unto thyself wrath against the day of wrath and revelation of the righteous judgment of God; who will render to every man according to his deeds: To them who by patient continuance in well doing seek for glory and honour and immortality, eternal life: But unto them that are contentious, and do not obey the truth, but obey unrighteousness, indignation and wrath, tribulation and anguish, upon every soul of man that doeth evil, of the Jew first, and also of the Gentile; but glory, honour, and peace, to every man that worketh good, to the Jew first, and also to the Gentile: For there is no respect of persons with God.

For over six thousand years God's righteous indignation and wrath has been held back. Satan's accusations and actions have been allowed to fully unfold for all to see their results and to see the contrast of God's longsuffering, loving, and patient character. All will fully understand why sin can never be allowed to enter the world again. God the Father has been blamed for the evil that Satan brought upon this earth and its inhabitants.

Now, since His Son paid the price, He can rightly and justly discipline the wicked. The seven last plagues have been a long time in coming. This wrath of God is for the wicked and is not directed toward God's people. Right after John announces the seven plagues, he writes about the safety of God's people standing on the sea of glass. This insertion by the Revelator is not to imply that the people of God are not on earth when the plagues fall, for we read that "no man was able to enter into the temple, till the seven plagues of the seven angels were fulfilled" (Rev. 15:8). However, it shows us that God's people will be protected just as the plagues that fell on the Egyptians did not harm the Israelites.

God's justice and wrath is about to be poured out on a stubborn, defiant, and wicked people without mercy. And while the wicked will be crying and gnashing their teeth, the righteous will be able to sing the song of victory. These plagues are what Isaiah 28:21 referred to when he wrote, "For the Lord shall rise up ... he shall be wroth ... that he may do his work, his strange work; and bring to pass his act, his strange act."

God is love and He is longsuffering, but He is also righteous and just. As we saw in the beginning of this study, God created a perfect world. The wickedness of humanity has caused complete degradation of all that was perfect. Satan's scheme did not elevate or better the angels or human beings. When sin is allowed to run its full course, it will be seen for the lie it is. Physical, mental, and spiritual decay and corruption is spawned by and is the result of deprivation of a personal relationship with the Creator. Peace and harmony is achieved only with God's brand of love. It's the only way.

Now let's turn to Revelation 16. In this chapter we read about the pouring out of the plague vials "upon the men which have the mark of the beast, and ... worshipped his image." Then, moving into chapter 17, we learn about the reasons for judgment. I want to spend some time looking at this chapter because in so doing I believe we can better understand and bring these closing events of earth's history into focus as to why these judgments have been so long in coming. Like Daniel 2 the angel gives the symbolic interpretation of what was seen. In this case, let's just go to the interpretation by the angel for this "great whore that sitteth upon many waters" with a name on her forehead that read "MYSTERY, BABYLON THE GREAT, THE MOTHER OF HARLOTS AND ABOMINATION OF THE EARTH" (Rev. 17:1, 5).

She is said to be "drunken with the blood of the saints, and ... the martyrs of Jesus" (verse 6). Under the fifth seal of Revelation 6:9, 10, we read about this same power that slays God's people and their blood cries out to be avenged. Daniel 7:20 tells of this same power, and as we have seen by previous identification, this woman is an apostate false religion, which points to the Roman Catholic Church. The horns are kingdoms, and by riding on this beast or its multiple powers, the church gave these kings the "divine right" to rule. The church controlled the secular world ruled by these kings. In 1825, on the occasion of a papal jubilee, Pope Leo XII struck a medal bearing on one side his own image and on the other that of a "woman" holding in her left hand a cross and in her right a cup with the legend around her "Sedet super Universum"—the whole world is her seat. Being the mother of harlots indicates that there are other apostate churches that together with her make up Babylon the great.

Why should John wonder "with great admiration" or "wonder with great wonder" as read in the original manuscripts (Rev. 17:6)? He had seen and was part of pagan Rome's persecution before Constantine's conversion, but now he is seeing into the future and witnessing the persecution of God's people by a professedly "Christian" church. She is persecuting the followers of the Lamb, and she is "drunk" with their blood. This wasn't admiration as we use the term, but astonishment or amazement that John expressed because he couldn't believe what he was seeing.

The beast is described as "was, and is not; and shall ascend out of the bottomless pit, and go into perdition" (verse 8). It had seven heads and ten horns. This describes Rome in its three phases: initially pagan and oppressive, a the wild beast that persecuted God's people; then it become a "Christian" church under the banner of Constantine, it briefly lost some of its ferocious and secular/civil persecuting character; lastly, before the end, it will revert and again assume its bloodthirsty and oppressive character.

The explanation of the seven heads, which is a part of the symbol, represent the seven mountains upon which the woman (church) sits. The beast is the same entity that gives the woman her power. He "was" ruler of this world by default of Adam. He "is not" when Christ reclaimed dominion at His death and resurrection. Yet "he is" because the judgment day is still in the future.

The ten horns are kingdoms, and John refers to the same vision he saw in Revelation 13, telling why the judgmental plagues had come upon this ecclesiastical body. Yes, she made all the nations/kingdoms to whom she gave power "drunk" with the deadly false "wine of her fornications" (doctrines).

In Revelation 18:2, 3 we read that "Babylon the great is fallen, is fallen ... For all nations have drunk of the wine of the wrath of her fornication." Revelation 19:20 adds, "And the beast was taken, and with him the false prophet that wrought miracles before him, with which he deceived them that had received the mark of the beast, and them that worshipped his image. These both were cast alive into a lake of fire burning with brimstone." Then Revelation 20:10 provides us with a final glimpse of the devil: "And the devil that deceived them was cast into the lake of fire and brimstone, where the beast and the false prophet are."

Yes, they will stand before God in the great white throne judgment scene, but their fate is here depicted along with all who are deluded by Satan, the adversary of all that is true.

Now to see the promised outcome of those who choose to repent and obey in submissive love to God and to their fellow human beings. These have the promised assurance and the previous history that God is able to protect them from dangers that are directed against others.

However, even though we have seen the reason for the plagues, let's return to Revelation 16 and study their future effects upon the earth and wicked mankind before seeing the glorious state of the redeemed.

In considering the seven last plagues, remember that there are similarities with those Pharaoh brought against himself and Egypt when Moses requested that he let the Israelites go. The first plague was poured out upon the earth and "there fell a noisome and grievous sore upon the men which had the mark of the beast" (Rev. 16:2). Remember, none fell on God's people. The second plague was poured out upon the sea, which became blood, and all living things in the sea died. The third plague was poured "upon the rivers and fountains of water; and they became blood" (verse 4). The angels declare that God's judgments are true and righteous because the wicked have shed the blood of the prophets and saints.

The fourth plague was poured "upon the sun; and power was given unto him to scorch men with fire. And men were scorched with great heat, and blasphemed the name of God ... and they repented not to give him glory" (verse 9). The fifth plague was poured out upon "the seat of the beast; and his kingdom was full of darkness; and they gnawed their tongues for pain, ... and repented not of their deeds" (verses 10, 11). Like Pharaoh, their hearts are totally hardened against God. Also like Satan they have reached the point of no return.

The sixth plague is poured out on "the great river Euphrates; and the water thereof was dried up, that the way of the kings of the east might be prepared" (verse 12). Also under this plague we find that "three unclean spirits like frogs come out of the mouth of the dragon, ... the beast, and ... the false prophet" (verse 13).

These three gather the kings of the earth and the whole world "to the battle of that great day of God Almighty" at a place called Armageddon (verse 14). These three unclean spirits are from the dragon (paganism), the beast (Roman Catholicism), and the false prophet (apostate Protestantism). These are unclean spirits and not the Spirit of the living God. First John 4:1 says, "Beloved, believe not every spirit, but try the spirits whether they are of God: because many false prophets are gone out into the world." Paul wrote to Timothy and reminded him of the dangers of false prophets and doctrines: "Now the Spirit speaketh expressly, that in the latter times some shall depart from the faith, giving heed to seducing spirits, and doctrines of devils; speaking lies in hypocrisy" (1 Tim. 4:1, 2); and "for the time will come when they will not endure sound doctrine; but after their own lusts shall they heap to themselves teachers, having itching ears; and they shall turn away their ears from the truth, and shall be turned unto fables. But watch thou in all things" (2 Tim. 4:3–5).

Modern spiritualism will be a player in all these agencies to bring together the forces of the world into the place called Armageddon. As we noted when we found King Saul turning to the witch of Endor, this is not acceptable to God. Why? Basically, when one seeks instruction from such sources, they are seeking truth from a liar. But most importantly, they are giving homage to Satan rather than the true God, the revealer of secrets and the source of all wisdom.

Since spiritualism supposedly contacts the dead, let's explore the doctrine of death. God told Adam and Eve that they would die if they ate from the tree of knowledge of good and evil (Gen. 2:17). Earlier in this study we found that Christ is "the Lamb slain from the foundation of the world" (Rev. 13:8). Adam and Eve died spiritually at the moment they ate the fruit, but they did not physically die for many years. Christ's self-sacrificial offering paid their death penalty just as it does ours. Paul said in Acts. 17:25–28 that God "giveth to all life, and breath, and all things; ... For in him we live, and move, and have our being."

Jesus called death a "sleep," when He said of Lazarus, "Our friend Lazarus sleepeth" (John 11:11). A few chapters earlier in John, Jesus states, "Marvel not at this: for the hour is coming, in the which all that are in the graves shall hear his voice, and shall come forth; they that have done good, unto the resurrection of life; and they that have done evil, unto the resurrection of damnation" (John 5:28, 29).

In Acts 2:29, 34 it was written concerning David that "he is both dead and buried, and his sepulchre is with us unto this day.... For David is not ascended into the heavens." Following are a number of other verses that shared the truth about death and the resurrection:

> Blessed and holy is he that hath part in the first resurrection: on such the second death hath no power. (Rev. 20:6)

> For the living know they shall die: but the dead know not any thing, neither have they any more a reward; for the memory of them is forgotten. Also their love, and their hatred, and their envy, is now perished; neither have they any more a portion for ever in any thing that is done under the sun. (Eccl. 9:5, 6)

> The soul that sinneth, it shall die. (Ezek. 18:4)

These verses clearly show that the dead are in their graves and they have no present influence or contact with the living or the dead. They all wait in their graves (not heaven or hell) until Jesus returns, at which time those who have chosen to follow God will be raised to receive their reward of eternal life: "Whosoever believeth in him should not perish, but have everlasting life" (John 3:16). "For, behold, the day cometh, that shall burn as an oven; and all the proud, yea, and all that do wickedly, shall be stubble: and the day that cometh shall burn them up, saith the LORD of hosts, that it shall leave them neither root nor branch.... for they shall be ashes under the soles of your feet in the day that I shall do this, saith the LORD of hosts."

The dead cannot speak at séances or cause tears from the eyes of paintings or statues to fall, and they cannot do the miracles it is claimed that they perform, such as healings. But what power can? As we have been reading, it is the dragon, that old serpent, Satan, who can deceive by many miracles. Remember, in Matthew 7:21–23, Jesus said, "Not every one that saith unto me, Lord, Lord, shall enter into the kingdom of heaven; but he that doeth the will of my Father which is in heaven. Many will say to me in that day, Lord, Lord, have we not prophesied in thy name? and in thy name have cast out devils? and in thy name done many wonderful works? And then will I profess unto them, I never knew you: depart from me, ye that work iniquity." In Matthew 24:24 Jesus said, "For there shall arise false Christs, and false prophets, and shall shew great signs and wonders; insomuch that, if it were possible, they shall deceive the very elect."

What have we learned about the dead? "You shall not surely die" was Satan's lie to Eve, but as soon as she disobeyed God's command, death was introduced into the world. All who have died are still in their graves awaiting the resurrections, whether it is the first or second. None of the dead have thoughts nor can they have any active part in today's events or in people's lives. Only God has immortality.

Now that we have determine the state of the dead, let's return to the discussion of the unclean spirits that are assembling their forces to fight against God in the battle of Armageddon.

They are interrupted by the pouring out of the seventh plague and the announcement, "Behold, I come as a thief" (Rev. 16:15). It is imperative that one understands from the way Revelation is written that there are "trees that make up the forest." One can only see the "details" by focusing upon one scene/event at the time. Even then, it is necessary to revisit each even to place it in the proper setting of the whole.

Revelation 16:14–16 sets this as occurring when the sixth plague is poured out upon the area of the Euphrates River. The pouring out of the vial takes place, but the "battle" is not until after the second resurrection when those forces are resurrected and surround the New Jerusalem.

Returning back to Revelation 17:16, we read that these ten horns (kings) "shall make her desolate and naked, and shall eat her flesh, and burn her with fire." We know that it is in the future as it is said in verse 14 that "these shall make war with the Lamb ... for he is Lord of lords, and King of kings." This time can only be when He ceases His intercessory priestly duties at the close of probation. This harlot (Babylon), again, refers to the apostate Catholic Church and her daughters, the Protestant churches.

In Revelation 18 we are given more details of the three angels' messages than was seen in chapter 14. The declaration that "Babylon the great is fallen" (Rev. 18:2) and "the earth was lightened with his glory" (verse 1) is not a literal fall, but a spiritual fall. God's people are summoned to "come out of her, my people, that ye be not partakers of her sins, and that ye receive not of her plagues" (verse 4). This fall is also after 1844 when the first angel began to sound the judgment hour message and before the pouring out of the plagues that are here being warned against and are to occur during earth's final days.

The cry to "come out of her, my people," is being heeded today. The merchandise that has been presented as "genuine" isn't being bought. The false doctrines, the lure of fornication, the lusts of the flesh and of the eyes, and the pride of life, as well as the luxuries of this world, are being seen for what they are. God's people are leaving the false institutions of Babylon. God's people are being sealed. The pleading voice of Jesus and the church and the light of the gospel shall not be heard anymore (Rev. 18:23), for time will soon be no more.

It is reported in Revelation 18:8 that "her plagues [will] come in one day." In Isaiah 34:8 it suggests that the plagues will fall in the space of a year: "For it is the day of the Lord's vengeance, and a year of recompenses for the controversy of Zion."

The seventh angel poured out his vial in the air, and there came a great voice out of the temple of heaven from the throne, saying, "It is done" (Rev. 21:6). Therefore, with the finishing of the cleansing of the heavenly sanctuary, the closing of probation (no more time to repent), and the sealing of God's people, the time of Christ's return is about to happen.

When Christ does return, the righteous will rejoice while the wicked will shudder in fear, for judgment will officially arrive in the form of eternal death:

> And I saw heaven opened, and behold a white horse; and he that sat on him was called Faithful and True, and in righteousness he doth judge and make war.... And he was clothed with a vesture dipped in blood: and his name is called The Word of God.... And he hath on his vesture and on his thigh a name written, KING OF KINGS AND LORD OF LORDS. And I saw an angel standing in the sun; and he cried with a loud voice, saying to all the fowls ... Come and gather yourselves together unto the supper of the great God; that ye may eat the flesh of kings ... captains ... mighty men, and ... horses, and of them that sit on them, and the flesh of all men, both free and bond, both small and great.... And the remnant were slain with the sword of him that sat upon the horse, which sword proceeded out of his mouth: and all the fowls were filled with their flesh. (Rev. 19:11–21)

Chapter 9
Behold, I Come Quickly

The Second Coming

With the second coming of Christ, the wicked are slain. Since there is no one to bury them, they become "supper" for the fowls of the air. Notice, 2 Thessalonians 2:8–12, "And then shall that Wicked be revealed, whom the Lord shall consume with the spirit of his mouth, and shall destroy with the brightness of his coming: Even him, whose coming is after the working of Satan with all power and signs and lying wonders, and with all deceivableness of unrighteousness in them that perish; because they received not the love of the truth, that they might be saved. And for this cause God shall send them strong delusion, that they should believe a lie: that they all might be damned who believed not the truth, but had pleasure in unrighteousness."

Let's pick up where we left God's people and bring them to this point in time. God's people have been spreading the three angels' messages with a loud voice. A call has gone out to "come out of her, my people, that ye be not partakers of ... her plagues" (Rev. 18:4). Because of this, we find that a death penalty has been imposed on all who do not worship the beast or his image and have their mark, which has been shown to be Sunday worship. Therefore, those who obey and keep God's commandments and reverence His holy seventh-day Sabbath, Saturday, are sealed and kept from harm. As the decree is about to be put into effect, the last or seventh trumpet sounds. "And there were great voices in heaven, saying, The kingdoms of this world are become the kingdoms of our Lord, and of his Christ; and he shall reign for ever and ever" (Rev. 11:5). The seventh seal has been opened as we read in Revelation 8:1: "There was silence in heaven about the space of half an hour."

In Acts 1:11 we read what the angel said to those who watched Christ ascend into heaven after His resurrection. "Ye men of Galilee, why stand ye gazing up into heaven? This same

Jesus, which is taken up from you into heaven, shall so come in like manner as ye have seen him go into heaven." There will be silence in heaven because all His holy angels will be coming with Him. When Christ appears in the clouds of glory, there will be a special resurrection, for Revelation 1:7 declares, "Behold, he cometh with clouds; and every eye shall see him, and they also which pierced him: and all kindreds of the earth shall wail because of him."

Matthew penned these words regarding Christ's return: "And he shall send his angels with a great sound of the trumpet, and they shall gather his elect from the four winds, from one end of heaven to the other" (Matt. 24:31). "When the Son of man shall come in his glory, and all the holy angels with him, then shall he sit upon the throne of his glory: and before him shall be gathered all nations: and he shall separate them one from another, as a shepherd divideth his sheep from the goats" (Matt. 25:31, 32).

Paul wrote this about the Lord's return:

For the Lord himself shall descend from heaven with a shout, with the voice of the archangel, and the trump of God: and the dead in Christ shall rise first: then we which are alive and remain shall be caught up together with them in the clouds, to meet the Lord in the air: and so shall we ever be with the Lord. (1 Thess. 4:16, 17).

Behold, I shew you a mystery; we shall not all sleep, but we shall all be changed, in a moment, in the twinkling of an eye, at the last trump: for the trumpet shall sound, and the dead shall be raised incorruptible, and we shall be changed. For this corruptible must put on incorruption, and this mortal must put on immortality. So when this corruptible shall have put on incorruption, and this mortal shall have put on immortality, then shall be brought to pass the saying that is written, Death is swallowed up in victory. (1 Cor. 15:51–54)

We can readily see from these verses that Christ's second coming is anything but secret. That is, He will *not* come and go and leave the living wicked to wonder where the "others" went. "Every eye shall see him" (Rev. 1:7).

There will be a lot of noise associated with His coming such as the shout of the archangel and the trumpet. Did you notice that the sky will be filled with ascending people? The righteous dead with their mortal, corruptible bodies will ascend to meet Jesus, and on the way, "in the twinkle of an eye," their vile bodies will put on incorruptibility and immortality. This group comprises the redeemed of all ages. This is the first resurrection, and the living righteous are caught up with the righteous who have been raised to life.

The living wicked are slain by the brightness of His coming and His presence, and the wicked dead remain in their graves. This is the harvesting of the wheat and the tares. Christ will return to take His children to the marriage supper of the Lamb.

We have just seen that the wicked become supper for the fowls of the air, but there is more. Notice that besides the physical torture that these plagues inflict upon the wicked persons, there is an equally devastating effect on nature as we read in Revelation 16. The seas and rivers became blood, the sun scorches, and then there is darkness, followed by drought, and a great earthquake, with the islands and mountains vanishing, and finally, the falling of enormous hailstones. Remember, the sixth seal depicts this scene:

And the heaven departed as a scroll when it is rolled together; and every mountain and island were moved out of their places. And the kings of the earth, and the great men, and the rich men, and the chief captains, and the mighty men, and every bondman, and every free man, hid themselves in the dens and in the rocks of the mountains; and said to the mountains and the rocks, Fall on us, and hide us from the face of him that sitteth on the throne, and from the wrath of the Lamb: For the great day of his wrath is come; and who shall be able to stand? (Rev. 6:14–17)

The Millennium and the Wicked

At this point we have come to Revelation 20, where Christ has come and taken the redeemed to heaven and Satan and his angels are left on this devastated planet. This chapter records the thousand years:

And I saw an angel come down from heaven, having the key of the bottomless pit and a great chain in his hand. And he laid hold on the dragon, that old serpent, which is the Devil, and Satan, and bound him a thousand years, and cast him into the bottomless pit, and shut him up, and set a seal upon him, that he should deceive the nations no more, till the thousand years should be fulfilled: and after that he must be loosed a little season.

And I saw thrones, and they sat upon them, and judgment was given unto them: and I saw the souls of them that were beheaded for the witness of Jesus, and for the word of God, and which had not worshipped the beast, neither his image, neither had received his mark upon their foreheads, or in their hands; and they lived and reigned with Christ a thousand years. But the rest of the dead lived not again until the thousand years were finished. This is the first resurrection. Blessed and holy is he that hath part in the first resurrection: on such the second death hath no power, but they shall be priests of God and of Christ, and shall reign with him a thousand years.

And when the thousand years are expired, Satan shall be loosed out of his prison, and shall go out to deceive the nations which are in the four quarters of the earth, Gog, and Magog, to gather them together to battle: the number of whom is as the sand of the sea. And they went up on the breadth of the earth, and compassed the camp of the saints about, and the beloved city: and fire came down from God out of heaven, and devoured them. And the devil that deceived them was cast into the lake of fire and brimstone, where the beast and the false prophet are, and shall be tormented day and night for ever and ever.

And I saw a great white throne, and him that sat on it, from whose face the earth and the heaven fled away; and there was found no place for them. And I saw the dead, small and great, stand before God; and the books were opened: and another book was opened, which is the book of life: and the dead were judged out of those things which were written in the books, according to their works. And the sea gave up the dead which were in it; and death and hell delivered up the dead which were in them: and they were judged every man according to their works. And death and hell were cast into the lake of fire. This is the second death. And whosoever was not found written in the book of life was cast into the lake of fire. (Rev. 20:1–15)

This chapter concerning the millennium gives us a lot of insight into what will be going on in the lives of God's people and Satan and his evil angels during the thousand years in heaven. Satan is said to be "chained" and cast into "the bottomless pit." This is not a literal chain or prison, but a "chain of circumstances." We say we are "chained" to a lot of things. This is a symbolic chaining. He could "deceive the nations no more, till the thousand years should be fulfilled" (Rev. 20:3). Why? The righteous are in heaven and out of his reach, and the wicked are all dead and will not be resurrected until the end of the 1000 years. Satan is restricted to this planet; he is not allowed in heaven nor is he allowed to go to any other planet that may be inhabited by God's created beings. He is here on a totally destroyed earth with only his fallen angels. He has a thousand years to contemplate what havoc his rebellion has caused. He had boasted that he could improve upon God's plan of love and rule the heavens and earth better than the Creator. Now for a thousand years he must face the consequences of his choices.

Satan and his angels know what fate awaits them. In Matthew 8:29 the devils that possessed the two men cried out to Jesus, "What have we to do with thee, Jesus, thou Son of God? Art thou come hither to torment us before the time?" And in 2 Peter 2:4 we read, "For if God spared not the angels that sinned, but cast them down to hell, and delivered them into chains of darkness, to be reserved unto judgment."

Just imagine, if you will, Satan during this thousand years sitting upon the rubble of that fallen city of Babylon, which caused the wicked to worship him, contemplating what went wrong. And at the end of the thousand years, Satan, along with all the wicked, will bow the knee to God and acknowledge that He is Lord, but like so many today, the mind is still in rebellion. Isaiah 45:23, Romans 14:11, and Philippians 2:9–11 state that every knee will bow before Christ and everyone will acknowledge that He is God. As humans we often think that we are "leaders" or the ones with the last word, but we forget that we are followers of either Christ or Satan. Will we follow Satan into the lake of fire or Christ into the heavenly realm?

It is said of the wicked, "They were judged every man according to their works" (Rev. 20:13). Now having been resurrected and judged, they are incited, by recently released Satan, to continue in the battle for which the three unclean spirits had gathered them. Satan now directs them to encompass "the camp of the saints about, and the beloved city" (Rev. 20:9). We will discuss what city this is in a little bit.

The Millennium and the Righteous

Here we need to review what the saints, the redeemed, the chosen of God, will be doing during the thousand years that Satan is bound and the earth is desolate. First, we saw that at Christ's second coming the righteous put on immortality, and with this proper attire they are worthy to go into the marriage supper of the Lamb. They chose the right path, the right course of action, the way, the truth, and the life. Each individual will have sifted through the record books of heaven and will be fully persuaded in their own minds that "true and righteous are thy judgments" (Rev. 16:7).

First Corinthians 6:2 states, "Do ye not know that the saints shall judge the world?" There will never be any doubt or question as to why any person was not redeemed or why a person was redeemed. Every mind will be fully satisfied that God is loving, merciful, kind, gracious, just, and longsuffering, and that only God is worthy of our praise, worship, adoration, and obedience. We will forever be loyal to Him. As it is written in Revelation 21:27, "And there shall in no wise enter into it [the New Jerusalem] any thing that defileth, neither whatsoever worketh abomination, or maketh a lie."

The New Heaven and New Earth

At the end of the thousand years, when all the necessary house cleaning has been laid to rest, when no more doubts can be raised, when every inquiring mind in heaven, those who lived on this earth and any extraterrestrial created beings by God anywhere have been fully satisfied, then the Holy City, the New Jerusalem will descend from heaven to earth. And it is then that Satan and his resurrected army of wicked will try to take control of the Holy City, but God will send fire down from heaven to destroy them and Satan will be cast into the lake of fire (Rev. 20:9). This is the purifying fire that is written about in 2 Peter 3:10–13: "But the day of the Lord will come as a thief in the night; in which the heavens shall pass away with a great noise, and the elements shall melt with fervent heat, the earth also and the works that are therein shall be burned up. Seeing then that all these things shall be dissolved, what manner of persons ought ye to be ... looking for and hasting unto the coming of the day of God, wherein the heavens being on fire shall be dissolved, and the elements shall melt with fervent heat? Nevertheless we, according to his promise [see Isa. 65:17], look for new heavens and a new earth, wherein dwelleth righteousness."

Revelation 21 begins with this verse: "And I saw a new heaven and a new earth: for the first heaven and the first earth were passed away." Here we see all the final stages of the great restoration of all things. "And he that sat upon the throne said, Behold, I make all things new. And he said unto me, Write: for these words are true and faithful." It's ironic, but the mockers and scoffers of God and His powers have ridiculed the creating ability of God. They have chosen to follow their own theories of evolution, and they will miss this great event the second time. In contrast, the believers who were not present at the first creation will be witnesses to this marvelous event and the recreation of the new earth.

Even though the righteous will have lived in heaven for a thousand years, their homes will be on the new earth, and the record says, "Behold, the tabernacle of God is with men, and he will dwell with them, and they shall be his people, and God himself shall be with them, and be their God" (Rev. 21:3). "And I saw no temple therein: for the Lord God Almighty and the Lamb are the temple of it. And the city had no need of the sun, neither of the moon, to shine in it: for the glory of God did lighten it, and the Lamb is the light thereof" (verses 22, 23).

Thus, we see what Jesus has revealed to John regarding the final fate of the redeemed and the wicked. John was in exile, and it looked hopeless for the gospel commission in which he had a part. But as we have seen all through the book of Revelation, when it looks bleak for God's children, God opens the door just a crack to reassure them that He is in charge and there is a merciful, just, and righteous end to this chaotic confusion that Satan's rebellion started. There will be no more suffering, tears, or death in the earth made new: "There shall be no more curse" (Rev. 22:3).

Recapitulation of Revelation's Events

Let's recap the events or some of the highlights we have seen in Revelation as they relate to this time in which we live, the final hours of earth's history. We were first introduced to the seven ages of the church, and we noted that we are living in the final age. This is represented by the Laodicean church, the lukewarm church, in which God's "professed people" are deceived into being not only in the world, but also being of the world. The stated intent of Cain, the Pharisees, and Saul when he was persecuting God's people was that they thought they were worshipping the God they believed they knew. But, as Jesus told James and John when they wanted to command fire down from heaven onto the Samaritans, He said, "Ye know not what manner of spirit ye are of" (Luke 9:55).

It is Satan who uses lies and force to maintain control. This last church will be subjected to and commanded to worship the beast or his image and receive his mark. They will think that they are "rich, and increased with goods, and have need of nothing," yet they are "wretched, and miserable, and poor, and blind, and naked" (Rev. 3:17). Three angels are sent with messages telling of God's coming judgment, and they give the everlasting gospel and warn against being a part of Babylon. Another angel calls for the people of God to come out of Babylon and not to partake in her false doctrines, which will result in suffering the last plagues.

Those who choose to escape are sealed by God, and when the last person is sealed as God's child, there will be a proclamation, "He that is unjust, let him be unjust still: and he that is filthy, let him be filthy still: and he that is righteous, let him be righteous still: and he that is holy, let him be holy still. And, behold, I come quickly; and my reward is with me" (Rev. 22:11, 12).

The last trumpet will sound and Christ will then return to take the righteous home. Satan and the wicked, along with this sin-cursed heaven and earth, will be destroyed by fire, and a new heaven and earth will be created wherein dwelleth righteousness. Wickedness and evil will have completely shown their end results. The last doubts of the validity of God's love will be forever erased. God's character will have been fully vindicated, and God's love, peace, righteousness, mercy, longsuffering, graciousness, and justice will forever be established in the redeemed.

Chapter 10
Some Misunderstood Teachings

Law and Grace

As we come to the close of this book, I want to examine God's doctrines or principles and the errors that have been brought into the Christian church. The Bible warns us to study God's Word in order to make sure we are following the truth. Paul wrote, "Study to shew thyself approved unto God, a workman that needeth not to be ashamed, rightly dividing the word of truth" (2 Tim. 2:15). Jesus said, "Search the scriptures; for in them ye think ye have eternal life: and they are they which testify of me" (John 5:39). Furthermore, it was written of the Bereans, "That they received the word with all readiness of mind, and searched the scriptures daily, whether those things were so" (Acts 17:11). It is also noted in the Old Testament, "To the law and to the testimony: if they speak not according to this word, it is because there is no light in them" (Isa. 8:20).

This verse by Isaiah is a good place to start our study. We have seen by it that "light" or "enlightenment" to God's will is made known by the law and the testimony of the Holy Spirit to the prophets by whom God chose to convey His messages. We have seen in our study of Daniel and Revelation that the beast power, the papacy, thinks that it can change God's laws, notably, the third and fourth commandments, with some alterations of the tenth commandment. The law prohibiting the making and worshipping of images was eliminated, the defining of the Sabbath was excluded to make it generic, and the law against coveting was divided to retain the correct number of commandments. The Sabbath was switched from the seventh day (Saturday), which God selected, sanctified, and blessed, to the first day of the week (Sunday), which the "church" set aside/chose.

We have explored the Sabbath question previously, but there is another aspect of the law that we haven't dealt with and that is the law in connection with grace. It is claimed that the Ten Commandments were done away with at Christ's crucifixion, but nine of them were restarted/re-instated in the New Testament. The Sabbath was just a Jewish day of worship, and Christians are to honor Christ's resurrection by worshipping on Sunday. The emphasis was placed on God's grace by being "under grace and not law." The law is said to be of the Jews. What is forgotten is that grace did not just begin with the crucifixion. We find that "Noah found grace in the eyes of the LORD" (Gen. 6:8). It was God's grace that preserved Job when Satan would have taken his life. But grace was before the world's foundation. His grace is shown in the giving of His Son, "The Lamb slain from the foundation of the world" (Rev. 13:8). "For God so loved the world, that he gave his only begotten Son, that whosoever believeth in him should not perish, but have everlasting life" (John 3:16). As we have seen, the daughters of the harlot or the Protestant churches, by continuing to teach the errors that they brought out of the Catholic Church, still pay homage to her.

Remember, when we studied Satan's fall and the origin of sin, we read that Lucifer tried to say that the problem wasn't with him, the problem was the law of God. The Ten Commandment law is described as follows: "the royal law" (James 2:8); "the law is holy" (Rom. 7:12); "the law is good" (1 Tim. 1:8); "perfect law of liberty" (James 1:25); "sin is the transgression of the law" (1 John 3:4); "The law of the LORD is perfect" (Ps. 19:7); "so speak ye, and so do, as they that shall be judged by the law of liberty" (James 2:12). By these verses, one can see that Satan, via his "agents"—human or institutions—are the bearers of false teachings.

No where is there any saving merits attributed to the keeping of the law. The function of the law is as Paul described, "a school master" that points out sin, a "glass" that shows the dirt on our face (Gal. 3:24; James 1:23–25). We have to go to the only Being who can "cleanse us from all unrighteousness" (1 John 1:9), the Promised One "slain from the foundation of the world" (Rev. 13:8), the crucified Savior, the only begotten Son of God, Christ Jesus. "For by grace are ye saved through faith; and that not of yourselves: it is the gift of God" (Eph. 2:8). It is the atoning blood by which one can achieve forgiveness and grace from God the Father, not the Decalogue!

Jesus said in Matthew 5:17, 18, "Think not that I am come to destroy the law, or the prophets: I am not come to destroy, but to fulfil. For verily I say unto you, Till heaven and earth pass, one jot or one tittle shall in no wise pass from the law, till all be fulfilled." At the heart of the old covenant was the Ten Commandments. The same is true of the new covenant, for we read, "For this is the covenant that I will make with the house of Israel after those days, saith the Lord; I will put my laws into their mind, and write them in their hearts: and I will be to them a God, and they shall be to me a people: And they shall not teach every man his neighbour, and every man his brother, saying, Know the Lord: for all shall know me, from the least to the greatest" (Heb. 8:10, 11).

The Ten Commandments continue to be at the heart of God's universe. These laws will not just be written upon stone and tucked away in the ark, but they will be written on our hearts and in our minds, and thus we will fulfill what is said in 1 John 5:1, 2: "Whosoever believeth that Jesus is the Christ is born of God: and every one that loveth him that begat loveth him also that is begotten of him. By this we know that we love the children of God, when we love God, and keep his commandments."

We refer to the old covenant as the one given in the Old Testament and the new covenant as the one instituted at the cross; however, if you think about it, the "new" covenant of the New Testament is actually the oldest one since it is ratified by the blood of the Lamb, who was slain from the foundation of the world. The "old" covenant is the newer one since it was ratified by the blood of animals on Mount Sinai. This old covenant was faulty, not because of God, but because of the children of Israel. They were to be a "holy nation," "a kingdom of priests," "a peculiar treasure" (Exod. 19:5–8), and all they had to do was to be obedient to God and keep His covenant. Unfortunately, they quickly forgot their promise to follow God and decided to do things their own way.

The people had been in bondage for many years. They knew of the God of Abraham, Isaac, and Jacob, and they had personally experienced the mighty power of God during the plagues of Egypt and in the crossing of the Red Sea, but they largely relied on their own strength. Their faith was weak, which is no excuse to sin and rebel, but it explains why they quickly slipped away from God and turned to a golden calf in hopes of being led back to Egypt. The general history of the nation of Israel follows a pattern of turning to God and then slipping away.

We have established that God is loving and gracious, and we are saved by His blood and grace. However, this does not diminish the law or our need to keep it. "For this is the love of God, that we keep his commandments: and his commandments are not grievous" (1 John 5:3). All who choose to obey can and will obey. As we read in Jeremiah 31:31, 32 and Hebrews 8:8–10, the new covenant was full of hope and promise. It is for each individual who chooses to follow it; it is ratified with Christ's blood; and it is the covenant of grace, justification, sanctification, and glorification.

As Ezekiel 14:14 teaches, every person will bear his own sin; we can only save ourselves by surrendering our will to God and accepting His grace. First Peter 2:9 states, "But you are a chosen people, a royal priesthood, a holy nation, God's special possession" (NIV). Christ died for each person who has ever lived that whoever believes in Him will obtain eternal life when He returns. He is a personal Savior that longs to come dwell in your heart if you will invite Him to do so (Rev. 3:20). He accepts all who totally surrender their will to Him. That's grace. The wages of sin is death. The law judges us, mercy pleads its case, and Jesus pays the penalty; therefore, God's gift of life is through grace. The law and grace are just two manifestations of God's character and are not contrary to each other.

Once Saved, Always Saved

There is a doctrine that is associated with salvation and its relationship to grace and the law that is prevalent and in error, and that is the concept of "once saved, always saved." The way it is presented implies that all one has to do is say the "sinner's prayer" and that person can never lose salvation. They can lose their "standing" but not their salvation. They can continue to sin because we no longer are "under the law," but are "under grace." This is Satan's subtle lie, and it is rebellion to continue indulging that little "sin which doth so easily beset us" (Heb. 12:1). Let's see what the Scriptures have to say. Please look up these words and phrases in your concordance and determine the true meaning of the doctrine of "once saved, always saved." None of these indicate that once the magic words of the sinner's prayer are uttered that that person can never change his mind. A person can accept or reject God's gift of grace on his deathbed. For example, one of the thieves on the cross accepted salvation while the other one rejected it.

Consider what the meaning of the following terms are in regards to "can I remain God's child if my actions are opposite of what these terms and phrases mean": born again; to the one that overcomes; abiding in Christ; believer; justified by faith; saved; choose you; laws written in hearts and minds; God's will and my will; obedience; saved by grace; etc.

What would have happened to Noah or any of his family had they chosen to abandon the ark prior to it resting upon dry land? Their fate would have been as the other persons during the flood. It is in the "abiding" that there is security. That isn't "works," but obedience. After we accept the gift of salvation, we need to continue to walk in His footsteps and follow God. The death of Jesus Christ upon the cross paid the price for every human being from Adam to today. However, it will be applied only to those who choose to confess, repent, and submit to the will of the Father.

It was stated from the beginning that salvation (redemption, restoration) was dependent on "the Lamb slain from the foundation of the world" (Rev. 13:8). That is grace and also the good news. Sin is an intruder; it did not have to occur, but since the possibility is inherent in "choice," the remedy was planned and executed before creation began. "Sin is the transgression of the law." Christ was tempted in every point as we are, but He did not sin (Heb. 4:15). "I'm only human" doesn't excuse sin, nor does "all have sinned" or "we can't keep from sinning." Sinning is a choice, either "to" or "not to," just as obedience is a choice. God does not save anyone against his will nor does He force anyone to be part of the loving and peaceful environment of the new earth. Most importantly, He will not accept an insincere "prayer" as if it were from the heart. "Be not deceived; God is not mocked: for whatsoever a man soweth, that shall he also reap" (Gal. 6:7). We can choose to change our minds. We can be deceived into believing a lie if we choose not to check it out or if it is something we choose to believe.

Saving faith is total obedience in the merits of Christ's redemptive blood and continually abiding in His will, laws, and love. The person who claims to be "saved" and continues to sin willfully, deceives himself. He is not born again. The born again person will not sin, "because he is born of God" (1 John 3:9; see also 1 John 2:1; 3:6; 5:18).

However, we do have an advocate that can restore us if we backslide and are genuinely repentant. But on the other hand, if we continually harden our hearts to the grieving of the Holy Spirit, we are in danger of crossing over the point of no return: "For it is impossible for those who were once enlightened, and have tasted of the heavenly gift ... if they shall fall away [by their choice], to renew them again unto repentance" (Heb. 6:4, 6).

Method of Baptism

Baptism was commanded by Christ as a memorial of the great facts of the gospel: "Go ye therefore, and teach all nations, baptizing them in the name of the Father, and of the Son, and of the Holy Ghost" (Matt. 28:19). In 1 Corinthians 5:3, 4 and Romans 6:3–9, our Savior's death, burial, and resurrection are typified in baptism. Baptism is for those who hear the gospel, believe, and repent. Repentance is necessary before one is baptized. Repentance is the acknowledging of a sinful life and nature and the turning away from continuing in those sins.

Romans 3:23 states, "For all have sinned, and come short of the glory of God." When the gospel is preached, the sinner recognizes his sinful condition and his condemnation by the righteousness of God's law as revealed in Christ. But when he accepts by faith the Lord Jesus Christ as his savior, he dies to sin and rises again in the newness of Christ's life in the faith of Jesus. "Therefore we are buried with him by baptism into death: that like as Christ was raised up from the dead by the glory of the Father, even so we also should walk in newness of life. For if we have been planted together in the likeness of his death, we shall be also in the likeness of his resurrection" (Rom. 6:4, 5).

Baptism is the outward expression of an inward experience and a newness in Christ. Without repentance and submission to God's will, one continues to exhibit the evil/wicked characteristics of our master Satan. Galatians 3:27 states, "For as many of you as have been baptized into Christ have put on Christ."

The only water baptism we find in Scripture is that by immersion, not sprinkling or another method (see Acts 8:38, 39; Matt. 3:16; Mark 1:5; John 3:23; Rom. 6:4, 5; Eph. 4:5; Col. 2:12). Since baptism emphasizes faith or belief, this precludes the baptizing of infants who are not able to believe in the Lord Jesus Christ for their salvation. It is in the knowledge and understanding of the fact that we are redeemed by God's grace in the accepting of Jesus' substitutionary blood that we have salvation. The act of baptism only attests to the fact that we believe this to be true and that the life we now live is in agreement with His principles. An infant can't do this, for its intelligence is insufficiently developed to comprehend the magnitude of such a decision. However, the act of baptism by itself only means you got wet and doesn't guarantee salvation. This magnifies the importance of the parent to "train up the child" in the true understanding of God. Therefore, when the child truly comprehends the sound doctrines/teachings of Scripture, the child can make that "right decision."

Christ is our example. At age twelve, He began going about His Father's business (Luke 2:42–49). At this young age He demonstrated insight, reasoning, and intelligence. "And all that heard him were astonished at his understanding and answers" (verse 47). However, it wasn't until He was thirty years old that He was baptized by John the Baptist: "Suffer it to be so now: for thus it becometh us to fulfil all righteousness" (Matt. 3:15).

Before one is baptized it is necessary for him to repent: "Repent, and be baptized every one of you in the name of Jesus Christ for the remission of sins" (Acts 2:38). There was no need for Jesus to repent because He had not sinned. His life proved we humans can keep God's holy law. He did not use His divinity to escape any of the temptations that came His way (Heb. 2:18; 4:15). We need that baptismal experience to bury the old man of sin and follow Christ's example.

We do not know the fate of children who die before the age of accountability, but we do have hints. God the Father knows the end from the beginning, and He is "not willing that any should perish, but that all should come to repentance" (2 Peter 3:9). Both Daniel and Revelation indicate that God foretells the events of the future and of our lives. He knows who will repent if given the opportunity. He knows the heart and the mind of every person on this planet. As parents we claim to want to do the best for our children, yet the condition of the world today is testimony that our children are following in worldly footsteps and not heavenly footsteps. We, as a society, have neglected to put God first in our lives; therefore, the societies of the world are crumbling and Babylon is falling.

Yes, it's time for true repentance and baptism. It is time to bury pride and lust and be willing to follow God and His laws and principles.

In Conclusion

We have touched on several topics during this study of Daniel and Revelation as they relate to understanding, as far as humanly possible, the overall conflict of good versus evil and our part in this drama. We have traced the consequences of good and evil from before there was evil to the near future when again there will be no evil. Satan blamed God for having a set of laws that blocked his prideful ambitions; Eve blamed the snake God made; Adam blamed God for the woman He gave him; and the world deteriorated from good to evil. God made provisions for such disobedience and self-delusion from before the creation of the world. It was God's great love, longsuffering, graciousness, mercy, and justice that has ever so slowly (in human time) been replaced by evil in order to show the end results of sin.

All can readily see the consequences that even the minutest sin would bring if allowed to flourish. However, in the new earth there will be no more sin: "And there shall in no wise enter into it [the new earth] any thing that defileth, neither whatsoever worketh abomination, or maketh a lie" (Rev. 21:27). The inhabitants of the new earth will have learned and are now practicing that which the inhabitants of this present earth, from Adam to the coming of Jesus, with the exception of the redeemed of all ages, refused to accept. That is, "Thou shalt love the Lord thy God with all thy heart, and with all thy soul, and with all thy mind. This is the first and great commandment. And the second is like unto it, Thou shalt love thy neighbour as thyself. On these two commandments hang all the law and the prophets" (Matt. 22:37–40; see also Deut. 6:5; 10:12; 30:6; Prov. 23:26; Mark 12:29–31; Luke 10:27; Lev. 19:18; Rom. 13:9; Gal. 5:14; James 2:8). This is summed up in the golden rule found in Matthew 7:12: "Therefore all things whatsoever ye would that men should do to you, do ye even so to them: for this is the law and the prophets."

Chapter 11
More Misunderstood Terms and Parables

Some Misunderstood Terms/Parables

The following terms and parables are often misunderstood. We will briefly examine them in this last chapter:

Soul
In the Old Testament the word "soul" is translated from the Hebrew *nehphesh*, which occurs 745 times in the original Hebrew. It is translated soul 473 times; life or lives 120 times; person 30 times; mind 16 times; heart 15 times; the dead and dead bodies 13 times; creature 9 times; will 4 times; appetite 2 times; lust 2 times; and thing 2 times. *Nehphesh* is translated in 43 different ways. In addition to the previous, it is rendered "breath," "beast," "fish," "desire," "ghost," "pleasure," etc. It is never translated "spirit," and it is never said to be "immortal."

Nehphesh (soul) is mortal and subject to death. Psalm 49:14 says, "Like sheep they are laid in the grave; death shall feed on them; and the upright shall have dominion over them in the morning; and their beauty shall consume in the grave from their dwelling. But God will redeem my soul from the power of the grave: for he shall receive me." Also, Isaiah 38:17 states, "Behold, for peace I had great bitterness: but thou hast in love to my soul delivered it from the pit of corruption: for thou hast cast all my sins behind thy back." *Nehphesh* (soul) may be "killed," "destroyed," etc. (see Gen. 17:14; Exod. 31:14; Josh. 10:30–39).

In the New Testament, "soul" comes from the Greek word *psuchee*, which occurs 105 times. It is translated life or lives 40 times, while some of the other translations render it "mind," "heart," "us," "you." Nowhere in the Bible is the soul (*psuchee*) said to be immortal, nor is it called a never-dying soul.

Spirit
The word "spirit" in the Old Testament occurs 234 times and is always translated from the Hebrew word *ruahh* (except for Job 26:4 and

Proverbs 20:27). *Ruahh* occurs 442 times and is translated 16 different ways. It is rendered spirit 232 times; wind 97 times; breath 28 times; smell 8 times; mind 6 times; blast 4 times; etc. *Ruahh* (spirit) is never said to be immortal. Another word translated "spirit" in the Old Testament is *n'shahmah*. It occurs 24 times and is translated breath 17 times; blast 3 times; spirit twice; soul once; and inspiration once.

In the New Testament, spirit is translated from the Greek word *pneuma* and occurs 385 times. It is translated spirit 291 times; ghost 92 times; wind once; and life once.

Therefore, we find the words in Hebrew and Greek that are translated "soul" in our English Bibles occur 923 times and "spirit" 827 times or 1750 times for both, but they are never modified by such expressions as "deathless," "never dying," or "immortal."

The Scriptures are clear. "The wages of sin is death; but the gift of God is eternal life" (Rom. 6:23).

Hell

The Hebrew word *sheol* is translated hell 31 times and pit 3 times. It is also translated grave 31 times. It refers to the place of or state of the dead: hell (Deut. 32:22; 2 Sam. 22:6; Job 11:8; Isa. 5:14; Jonah 2:2); grave (Gen. 37:35; 1 Kings 2:6, 9; Job 7:9; 24:19; Ezek. 31:15). In these texts it is clear that *sheol* is a place of rest, silence, secrecy, darkness, sleep, and corruption. Both righteous and wicked go to *sheol* (the grave or state of the dead) (Gen. 37:35; Num. 16:30, 33; Ps. 89:48). *Sheol* is the same as *hades* (Greek term) in the New Testament. *Hades* never means a place of punishment. It means "an unseen place," "the grave," "pit," "region of the dead" (see Matt. 11:23; 16:18; Luke 10:15; 16:23; Acts 2:27, 31; 1 Cor. 15:55; Rev. 1:18; 20:13, 14).

Gehenna is the Greek mode spelling of the Hebrew words "valley of Hinnon," and it refers to hell. In this valley the refuse of Jerusalem together with the bodies of animals was consumed. And that which the continual fire didn't destroy was consumed by worms. It is used as a symbol or type of slaughter and destruction. It is not a place where the wicked are now being punished or where they will be kept alive in endless torment (see Josh. 15:8; 18:16; 2 Kings 23:10; 2 Chron. 28:3; 33:6; Jer. 7:31, 32; 19:2, 6; 32:35; Matt. 5:22, 29, 30; 10:28; 18:9; 23:15, 33; Mark 9:43, 45, 47; Luke 12:5; James 3:6). It is clear from the use of this word that it refers to the lake of fire where the wicked will be destroyed.

Hades is the place of the dead, both righteous and wicked, from which they are brought only by a resurrection (Rev. 20:13). On the other hand, *gehenna* is the lake of fire into which the wicked will be cast alive after their resurrection and judgment and destroyed, body and soul (Matt. 10:28).

State of the Dead

This parable of the rich man and Lazarus (Luke 16:19–31) is one in a series of parables that started in Luke 13 with the mustard seed and ends with this one in chapter 16. It cannot be a literal description of the condition of man after death because we have just seen in the study of "soul and spirit" and "hell," and in "the state of the dead," that this would not be supported by those scriptures. We "don't go to Abraham's bosom"; "one drop of water" can't "cool" a man in hell; "people can't talk" back and forth between heaven and hell; and sinners are not punished until the day of judgment (see 2 Peter 2:9; John 5:28, 29; Rev. 22:12; 1 Thess. 4:13–18; Ps. 146:3, 4; Eccl. 9:5, 6, 10).

Do you really think that our loving, gracious, merciful, and just God would subject us, the redeemed, to daily seeing and hearing the torture of the wicked? We will not need that kind of an example to remind us not to sin and repeat this world's history. We will have a reminder of how awful and devastating sin is when we see those nail-scarred hands and feet that we caused and daily give praise for His unselfish, self-sacrificing love.

The teachings of the parable are as follows:

- In this life we settle our eternal destiny; the great gulf is fixed

- No man is valued merely for his possessions

- Most importantly, we should share the good news of the gospel with our loved ones (and the world) while we are alive

This parable and others texts are often quoted as evidence that at death a person either goes directly to heaven or hell. However, read 1 Corinthians 5:1–8 and Philippians 1:19–30. Both of these passages make it clear that Paul isn't speaking of immediately being "present with the Lord" at his death. The thought content of the verses does not convey that conclusion, and Paul's other writings do not support the idea that he believes differently from what the other scriptures express. Immortality is given at Christ's second coming, not at death (see 1 Cor. 15:51–54; 1 Thess. 4:13–18; Col. 3:4; 2 Tim. 4:8).

The thief on the cross is another event that is used as an example of a person going to heaven at death. Is it true? You can read the account in Luke 23:39–45. We know that when the Scriptures were written there were no punctuation marks. These were added later and were not inspired. The wording is correct, but there is a comma that is out of place, which causes Christ to become a liar. I don't think any believer would call our Lord a liar. If you put the comma where it belongs, after "today," then this text harmonizes with the rest of Scripture. See the use of "today" in Hebrews 3:7, 15; 4:7; and 5:5. On Sunday morning Jesus, at His resurrection, said to Mary, "I am not yet ascended to my Father" (John 20:17). The "today" in Jesus' conversation with the thief took place on Friday. The thief, nor Jesus, ascended to heaven when they died. The thief whom Christ promised eternal life will ascend to heaven on the day of resurrection.

First Peter 3:18–20 is also used out of context in an effort to persuade people to believe Satan's lie that death doesn't mean death, but eternal life. All have sinned and are, therefore, in the prison house of sin (see Rom. 7:14; Gal. 3:22; 5:16, 17; 2 Peter 2:19). When the Savior was on earth, He liberated prisoners from the prison of sin by His preaching and teaching (see Luke 4:16; Isa. 61:1; John 8:32, 36). Christ, by His Spirit, preached through Noah to the people in the prison house of sin in the days before the flood (2 Peter 2:5; Heb. 11:7; Rom. 8:1, 2; Gen. 6:3). The "spirits in prison" is not a reference to disembodied spirits (Heb. 12:9, 23; Num. 16:22; 27:16.) It is clear by these texts that the reference is to people alive on this earth. It is only in this life that a person has the ability and the opportunity to hear the gospel and choose to accept or reject salvation (Heb. 9:27; Eccl. 9:5, 10).

In the texts listed under the words used for Hell, it is clear there is no place now burning with the wicked nor will there be a perpetual place of burning in the future. What we see in Jude 7 is "Sodom and Gomorrha, and the cities about them in like manner, ... suffering the vengeance of eternal fire" (see also Deut. 29:23; 2 Peter 2:6; Gen. 19:24). The fires of their destruction have been extinguished for centuries, but as Deuteronomy 29:23 states, their end result is permanent, complete: "The whole land thereof is brimstone, and salt, and burning, that it is not sown, nor beareth, nor any grass groweth therein."

The eternal fire that destroyed those cities is the same eternal (everlasting, forever) fire that will destroy the wicked. The fire will not be extinguished or go out until it has accomplished the work assigned—that of complete destruction of the wicked, along with Satan and his evil angels. When we study the fate of the wicked and the state of the dead, we find that their eventual end will be ashes and no remembrance of former things will come to the minds of the redeemed. Therefore, an eternal presence of the wicked being punished is not possible, or our just and merciful God would be a mockery.

Summation

This brings us back to the beginning of this study. We find that we have a loving, just, gracious, merciful, longsuffering, kind, and everlasting God who planned every detail of a perfect world that would exist without end. There has been some interruption and marring of that perfect world, which was not by any fault of the Creator God, but by His created beings. Thus, we have been "a proving ground," if you please, of a great battle between the forces of good and the forces of evil. The good forces only use methods that equate to love, while the evil forces use "no holds barred" methods. And to complicate matters, the evil force can use good methods, but with evil intent.

God is true to His loving character. He is still reaching out His outstretched arms in love to all who will believe and accept His gift of salvation (Rom. 10:20, 21; Isa. 65:2). He doesn't take pleasure in the death of the wicked (Ezek. 18:23; 33:11). God did everything He could to prevent and make a way of escape for the guilty (1 Cor. 10:13). He loves each of us so much that He willingly took our place in death, and His plea is still heard: "Turn ye from your evil ways; for why will ye die?" (Ezek. 33:11). James 1:14, 15 reveals that a person is tempted by his own lusts. His lust then leads to sin, which ends in death. Solomon wrote in Ecclesiastes 12:13, "Let us hear the conclusion of the whole matter: Fear God, and keep his commandments: for this is the whole duty of man,"

We have explored this battle that rages within us and have seen its results as recorded in history and daily about us. It is our choice as to which side we choose to take our stand on. It is our soul (life) that we lose or keep. God's character has been vindicated. His principles of ruling through love are right and just and in the end it will result in peace. Who will you serve? The Creator—God—or the created—Satan? "Choose you this day" (Josh. 24:15).

It is our choice. I and those who had a part in this book hope and desire that through this text you will have a better understanding of the conflict between God and Satan and will choose to follow the Creator God. May you daily focus upon the Author and Finisher of our faith. "Behold, I come quickly: hold that fast which thou hast" (Rev. 3:11).

Remember, the good news of the gospel of salvation is free. It is a gift from God.

We invite you to view the complete
selection of titles we publish at:

www.TEACHServices.com

Scan with your mobile
device to go directly
to our website.

Please write or email us your praises, reactions, or
thoughts about this or any other book we publish at:

P.O. Box 954
Ringgold, GA 30736

info@TEACHServices.com

TEACH Services, Inc., titles may be purchased in bulk for
educational, business, fund-raising, or sales promotional use.
For information, please e-mail:

BulkSales@TEACHServices.com

Finally, if you are interested in seeing
your own book in print, please contact us at

publishing@TEACHServices.com

We would be happy to review your manuscript for free.

www.ingramcontent.com/pod-product-compliance
Lightning Source LLC
Chambersburg PA
CBHW081925170426
43200CB00014B/2831